Team Building:
Blueprints for Productivity and Satisfaction

D1009272

Team Building:
Blueprints for Productivity and Satisfaction

Edited by W. Brendan Reddy, Ph.D.
with Kaleel Jamison

Copublished by
NTL Institute for Applied Behavioral Science
and University Associates, Inc.

© 1988 NTL Institute for Applied Behavioral Science.

Printed in the United States of America
ISBN: 0-9610392-5-6

Library of Congress Cataloging-in-Publication Data

Team building.

    Bibliography: p.
    1. Work groups.   I. Reddy, W. Brendan, 1937–
II. Jamison, Kaleel.
HD66.T42   1988   658.4'02   88-1670
ISBN 0-9610392-5-6

This book is copublished by NTL Institute for Applied Behavioral Science, 1240 North Pitt Street Centre, Suite 100, Alexandria, Virginia 22314 and by University Associates, Inc., 8517 Production Avenue, San Diego, California 92121.

Some articles have been reprinted with permission from other sources. The first page of each article cites the holder of the copyright for that particular work. Some articles contain figures or tables reprinted with permission from other sources, which are cited below the reprinted material. To request permission to reprint material for which NTL Institute holds the copyright, write to the publications permissions department of NTL Institute at the address provided above.

Publications Manager, NTL Institute: Catherine A. Messina
Production Manager, University Associates: Margaret Levene

Dedication

Kaleel Jamison was excited about coediting a book on team building. We spent many spirited hours discussing—and arguing about—what and who should be included in this project. Despite Kaleel's illness and the knowledge that it was fatal, she continued to work on the book until her death on August 30, 1985.

Kaleel Jamison, a trainer and consultant, was a warm and dedicated professional who loved her work. She is sorely missed by her colleagues, friends, and clients. **Team Building: Blueprints for Productivity and Satisfaction** is dedicated to her memory.

W. Brendan Reddy, Ph.D.

Table of Contents

III. Applications

IV. Clients and Consultants

V. Multiculturalism

Introduction

Team building has come of age. While other types of training interventions have become passé, team building—in a variety of forms—has evolved into a frequent "intervention of choice."

Managers in both profit-making and not-for-profit organizations recognize the importance of quick responses to crises, thoughtful planning, and the full use of human resources in solving complex problems. Moreover, organizational subunits are becoming more interdependent, requiring teams of managers to work closely together. In addition, women and minority group members are gaining membership in these managerial teams. Developing and using the individual, interpersonal, and group skills required to produce a creative, wise, efficient, productive, and satisfying team is at best difficult. Team building is a response to this challenge.

The following 19 chapters address a wide range of team building issues and dynamics. Written for the team builder and the manager considering team building, this book was created in response to a need to feature **what is currently occurring** in the field, and thus is written by experts in the **practice** of team building.

Most of the chapters were written expressly for this book. The first three are classic articles that are reprinted here because they represent the best of the basic literature. A few others, adapted for this book, also appear in the current literature. Although the authors have diverse backgrounds, all but a few of these training professionals are members of NTL Institute for Applied Behavioral Science.

The book consists of five major sections, which are titled fundamentals, theory and dynamics, applications, clients and consultants, and multiculturalism.

In **Section I: Fundamentals,** the authors explore the basic components of the team building processes. W. Warner Burke focuses on the purpose of team building, setting goals, and analyzing how work is performed according to team members' roles and responsibilities. He examines the ways the team is working—its norms, decision making, and communications—and interteam relations. Each of the purposes is illustrated with examples and descriptions of techniques.

Thomas H. Patten, Jr., using detailed case studies of organizations vastly different in size and scope, tells us how to design the team building intervention as well as how to conduct it. He examines two cases and compares diagnoses, interventions, and results.

Section II: Theory and dynamics offers the reader chapters of varying breadth and depth on the theory and dynamics of team building, with both a macro and micro focus.

Marvin R. Weisbord describes team work as the "quintessential contradiction of a society grounded in individual achievement." To fully experience a productive community, he claims we must unlearn the "self-limiting assumptions about individual effort and authority that work against cooperation." Weisbord views team building as a way of learning necessary skills, pointing out that team building succeeds when the conditions of interdependence, leadership, and equal influence are met. He offers a model of team building and instructs us on the components.

Another model, the Team Performance Model, is presented and discussed by Allan B. Drexler, David Sibbet, and Russell H. Forrester. This model integrates the work of Jack R. Gibb with the theories of Arthur Young, and presents seven stages of group development, from orientation to renewal.

Gene Bocialetti demonstrates that emotions and emotional experiences are constantly present in organizational life. He contends that because emotions are inevitable, and because they can affect productivity and the quality of work life—for better or for worse—they must be managed. Bocialetti describes the impact of suppressing emotions on the work place, and finds the following three components crucial to managing affect in the organization: timing, context, and extent.

Nancy L. Brown discusses four illusions in team building, the "ROCS": rationality, objectivity, consciousness, and separability. She offers ways of dealing with their potential destructiveness, stressing that the consultant must always be aware of the presence of these illusions in the consultant's **own** mind. Brown further adds that once team members discuss the presence or absence of ROCS in their own work, the team can adjust its assumptions and move on to more productive work.

Philip G. Hanson and Bernard Lubin approach team building as group development, discussing the characteristics of a well-functioning team and giving a step-by-step description of the team building process and its various stages. They offer a basic assessment instrument for diagnosing a team's strengths and limitations, and emphasize that team building should not be a "one-shot event," but an ongoing process with continuous diagnosis, the planning and implementing of changes, evaluation of the changes, and modification of the program as indicated by the evaluation.

Jane Moosbruker contrasts the American approach to groups with that of the Japanese, demonstrating the need for a team leadership model that is practical for our industrial culture. She describes typical member behaviors and concerns that emerge during each phase of the model, and the appropriate leader behavior that must occur to facilitate group movement, and thus effectiveness and productivity.

The role of the creative outlook in team building is explored by John D. Adams. He attributes team disalignment to the ways in which we formulate our views of reality—that is, the beliefs, attitudes, values, and expectations moderating our behavior. Adams describes two "mindsets": the operational/reactive, in which the environment is allowed to dominate one's behavior, and the strategic/creative, in which one shapes events instead. The team building focus must be tied to the predominant outlook of the team, Adams suggests, or else team building must specifically intend to alter the team's outlook toward the strategic/creative mindset. With training and practice, team members can learn to recognize which outlook is predominant and to switch outlooks as needed.

Kathleen D. Dannemiller describes her work at Ford Motor Company, where she found that traditional team building concepts and practices enforced the separation and fragmentation of functional groups. She and her colleagues developed strategies to connect leaders of separate divisions, using basic team building concepts to benefit both divisions and the company. Dannemiller provides the model of the "arthritic" organization, in which movement at each juncture is blocked and people operate out of "arthritic boxes" isolating them by function. She describes a generic intervention involving organization members who had never before been in the same room at the same time.

Section III: Applications begins with Eva Schindler-Rainman's description of six trends calling for team work: shifting funding sources, the recruiting of teams, the move from "turfdom" to collaboration, the information society, the world of volunteers as a visionary force, and new populations. She notes both the positive and negative aspects of building teams, offering several strategies for composing voluntary system teams.

Robert T. Golembiewski illustrates ways of dealing with major differences when working with teams in both the public and private sectors. His experience leads him to find seven key areas in which typical organizations in business and government settings differ. Golembiewski discusses implications of these differences, providing an orientation for the public-sector consultant.

Section IV: Clients and consultants leads off with Judith D. Palmer's advice for the manager who must build a team: "Don't panic!" She reassures readers that although the concept of team building may seem intimidating, it is actually quite manageable for the manager. She outlines the stages a manager can expect the team to go through and a "basic triangle" of key elements that must be present for the team to do its work: task, team, and tools. Palmer's presentation clearly shows that team building is not only an ongoing process, but one in which the manager **must** play a pivotal role.

How to stay in charge during a team building effort despite hiring a consultant is discussed by Richard E. Byrd. He describes situations in which consultants come between bosses and their teams, thereby contributing more to the problem than to the solution. Byrd illustrates many ways in which consultants take over the process, advising managers of the pitfalls—and ways to avoid them—that can come with getting "help" from a consultant.

Herman Gadon identifies specific issues and a model dealing with the socialization of the newcomer to an ongoing work group. In his discussion, he notes ways to help managers and group members cope more effectively with these issues. Gadon moves us through the predictable process of group development—connecting, competing, collaborating, and caring—and gives advice for integrating new members more effectively at each stage.

Section V: Multiculturalism focuses on cultural issues—particularly gender and minority group considerations—in team building. Before a manager hires a team building consultant, Brendan Reddy and Carol Burke recommend that several areas be explored. Now that more women and minority members belong to management teams, the authors emphasize multicultural issues and suggest that managers conduct in-depth interviews with prospective consultants so that they can make well-informed hiring choices.

Susan L. Colantuono and Ava A. Schnidman focus on building multifunctional work teams. They contend that the issues of multifunctional teams differ from those of intact work groups, meaning that team building for these teams must also differ. The authors build their team sessions on six key goals: clarifying the mission, analyzing gaps and overlaps, unveiling specialties, dealing with stereotypes, easing communication, and empowering the group.

In the final chapter, Frederick A. Miller shows that team building is no longer a process **of** white men **for** white men. He describes the long-existing norms for teams and states that issues of racism and sexism must be addressed for teams to be effective and productive. Miller also points out the many pitfalls—subtle and obvious—that teams and managers must avoid or work through if they are to succeed.

I consider these works important contributions to the field of team building, and hope that they will prove informative and valuable to the readers.

W. Brendan Reddy, Ph.D.

Section I.
Fundamentals

Team Building

W. Warner Burke

When a work group has at least one goal that is common to all members and when accomplishment of that goal requires cooperative interdependent behavior on the part of all group members, team building may be an appropriate intervention. Dyer's (1977) three check lists are useful criteria for determining more specifically the appropriateness of team building for a work group. Studying his lists will help clarify the purposes and the nature of team building.

Using Beckhard's (1972) succinct statement of the four primary purposes of team building and Plovnick, Fry, and Rubin's (1975) elaboration as a guide, I shall now provide a more thorough explanation of team building. According to Beckhard (1972), there are four purposes of team building:

1. to set goals or priorities,
2. to analyze or allocate the way work is performed according to team members' roles and responsibilities,
3. to examine the way the team is working—that is, its processes, such as norms, decision making, communications, and so forth,
4. to examine relationships among the team members.

Beckhard points out that all these purposes are likely to be operating in a team building effort, "but unless **one** purpose is defined as **the** primary purpose, there tends to be considerable misuse of energy. People then operate from their own hierarchy of purposes and, predictably, these are not always the same for all members" (Beckhard 1972, p. 24). From a combination of responses to Dyer's check lists and individual interviews with group members, a diagnosis can be made that should indicate the primary purpose for an initial team building session. If the team building effort is the first for the group, the OD practitioner should determine if the focus of the first session should be setting goals or establishing priorities among team goals. If the goals and their priorities are clear, the OD practitioner should determine if the roles and responsibilities among team members are clear. If so, then the practitioner determines if working procedures and processes are clear. It is important and beneficial for the OD practitioner to use Beckhard's four purposes in the order that they are listed. The reason for this ordering of the purposes is as follows: **interpersonal** problems could be a consequence of group members' lack of clarity regarding team goals, roles, and responsibilities, or procedures and processes; problems with **procedures and processes** could be a consequence of group members' lack of clarity regarding team goals or roles and responsibilities; and problems with **roles and responsibilities** may be a result of group members' lack of clarity about team goals. To begin a team building effort with work on interpersonal relationships may be a misuse of time and energy, as it is possible that problems in this area are a result of misunderstandings in one of the other three domains. Clarifying goals, roles, and responsibilities, or team procedures and processes may eliminate certain interpersonal problems among team members; clarifying roles and responsibilities may in itself eliminate some of the problems with the team's working procedures and processes; and clarifying team goals and their priorities may in itself eliminate certain problems team members may have with their roles and responsibilities.

We shall now consider case examples of team building interventions for each of these four purposes.

Setting goals and priorities

In the course of an OD effort with a medical school, the school's internal consultant and I, an outside consultant, were asked by one of the clinical department chairs to help with some departmental team building. In our interviews with the department members, my colleague and I diagnosed that there was a pervasive sense of no direction for the department as a whole. In a subsequent meeting with the chairman, the three of us designed an off-site session for one evening and the following day for the 15 members of the department. Briefly, the design of this off-site meeting was as follows. The 15 members, including the chairman, were initially divided into three groups of five people each, heterogeneously grouped. Their common tasks were (1) to determine what they believed the departmental goals should be and (2) to select two of their members to represent them in a later plenary session. Having developed their goal statements, the three groups then assembled in the large room and the two representatives from each group met together in the center while the remaining nine department members were positioned around them as observers. Figure 1 depicts this arrangement of a small group of six

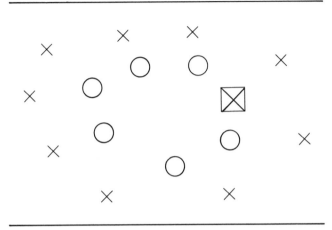

Figure 1. Configuration of the second phase of an off-site meeting to set departmental goals.

persons working together in the center, with their colleagues gathered around them and observing.

The task for this six-person temporary executive committee was to communicate what each group had developed and to consolidate their three lists of statements into one, which would then become the statement of objectives for the department. An empty chair was provided within this inner circle of six so that, if any of the observers believed that what her or his group had developed was not being represented or thought that this temporary executive committee was going astray, the person could occupy the empty chair, state her or his position or raise an issue, wait for and possibly deal with the reaction of the executive group, and then return to observer status.

Once the executive group had consolidated the three lists into one, the total group individually ranked the statements (14 in this case) according to priority of importance for the department. Next, the total group individually selected its first and second choices of objectives it wished to develop into action steps for implementation. The 15 people were then regrouped into three groups of five, according to their choices of an objective. These three groups met periodically after the off-site meeting to plan action steps for implementing the three most important objectives.

At the conclusion of the off-site meeting, each person was asked to respond to two questions, with responses arranged according to a five-point Likert scale: (1) How pessimistic or optimistic are you at the moment about the state of the department? (The 1-5 response ranged from "highly pessimistic" to "highly optimistic.") (2) To what extent do you believe positive change will occur as a result of this meeting? (The 1-5 response ranged from "not at all" to "to a great extent.") I like to ask these two questions toward the end of an off-site meeting because they provide a relatively simple way to consider the process of the meeting— people's feelings—and an opportunity to examine the degree of an individual's motivation to follow through on the steps planned for future implementation. In this case the departmental members' ratings were uniformly optimistic and positive.

The rationale for such a team building design has several elements. For such a short period of time (in this case only slightly more than one day), it is important to have as much member participation as feasible and to use the allotted time as efficiently as possible. The smaller group of six obviously could work more efficiently than the total group of 15, but some degree of total participation was maintained by employing the empty chair. Selecting representatives and then being able to see what they do, and also having a chance to influence their decision making, helps ensure the involvement of all department members and therefore their commitment to implementing the goals they identified. The follow-up groups did indeed meet periodically to plan action steps. A year later, in a brief interview, my colleague and I were pleased to learn that the department chairman continued to be satisfied with the progress of his department. He attributed much of this progress to the success of the off-site meeting.

Allocating work according to roles and responsibilities

Ambiguity regarding one's role and conflict between what is expected of an individual in a particular role and what that individual believes is appropriate can cause considerable confusion within a work group and anxiety for its members (Katz & Kahn, 1978). There are various techniques for gaining greater clarification of roles and responsibilities within a team. These techniques typically involve team members' (1) presenting their perceptions and understandings of their roles to one another, (2) discussing these perceptions and understandings, and (3) modifying roles as a function of increased agreement about mutual expectations. One such technique is the role analysis technique developed by Dayal and Thomas (1968). Another similar one is the job expectation technique, which is particularly useful when there is a need to integrate a new member into a team (Huse, 1980).

A technique that is particularly suitable for situations of role conflict is Harrison's (1972) role negotiation technique. Although it is most suitable for this second purpose of team building, the approach also may be used with either of the remaining two purposes, since role is not limited to formal position. According to Harrison (1972), this role negotiation technique "intervenes directly into the relationships of power, authority and influence within the group" (p. 92). Each group member lists for each other member the things these other members (1) should do more or better, (2) should do less or stop, and (3) should continue as now. Agreements about changes are negotiated among the members and then finalized in the form of a written contract.

A technique that emphasizes the responsibilities aspect of this second purpose of team building is what Beckhard and Harris (1977) refer to as **responsibility charting**. Using a grid format, the types of decisions and actions that need to be taken are listed along the left side and those who should have some part in the decision-making process are listed across the top of the grid. Figure 2 shows this type of grid. The process consists of assigning an action to each of the team members whose names appear opposite an issue or decision. As the exhibit shows, there are the following four types of actions: R, the **responsibility** to

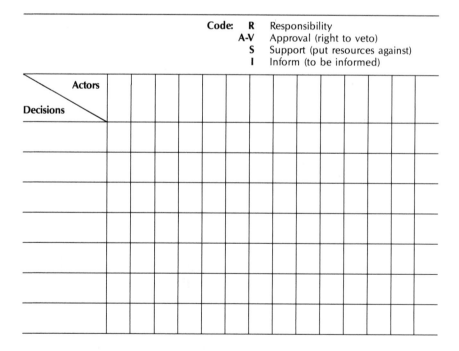

Figure 2. Responsibility chart
(Beckhard/Harris, *Organizational Transitions: Managing Complex Change,* ©
1977 Addison-Wesley Publishing Company, Inc., Reading, Massachusetts. Page 78,
Figure 2. Reprinted with permission.)

ensure action, to ensure that the decision is implemented; A-V, **approval** required or the right to **veto**; S, provide logistical **support** and resources; and I, must be **informed** about the decision or action. As Beckhard and Harris point out, there can be only one R on any single horizontal line. Either a consensus is reached by the team, or the boss determines who takes the responsibility.

Responsibility charting is particularly useful for new teams and for start-up situations. The process can also be used for problem solving in an ongoing team. Beckhard and Harris describe a case in which the top management team of a regional headquarters of an oil company had been having difficulty for several years in working out a new franchise relationship with some of the company's gas station owners:

> The problem was complex, and there had been all sorts of misun-derstandings, conflicts, slowdowns, and differences of emphasis between staff areas. The top management—the managing director, director of marketing, director of operations and director of finance—were concerned about this issue because it was a matter of significant investment and cost, but they had been unable to resolve it . . . . It was suggested that they do a responsibility chart-ing exercise on the problem, which they did. As a result, they discovered that they did not have a consensus about the location of the different types of responsibilities and behaviors. This prob-lem was relatively easy to work through (Beckhard and Harris 1977, p. 82).

Examining team procedures and processes

The third purpose of team building is to establish working procedures and processes for a newly formed team or to examine and look for ways of improving these procedures and processes if the team has already been operating as a group for some time. By **processes**, Beckhard (1972) means such things as group norms and leadership style. **Procedures** are the processes that are more directly related to goal (task) accomplish-ment, such as type of decision making, problem-solving technique, com-munication, and team structure for dealing with different agenda. The team building activity therefore involves (1) identifying the norms that are hindering effective team work and (2) changing them to different norms that will facilitate teamwork. The activity may be examining a particular team procedure that doesn't seem to be working very well. Table 1 presents a brief report of a case in which the communication procedure within a team was vastly improved by first examining the nature of the problem and then planning and implementing a new pro-cedure for internal communications.

Table 1
The Case of the Misunderstood Memo*

Recently, a vice president in a large U.S. corporation was having trouble with his division managers occasionally responding inappropriately to his memos. The vice president had the choice of (a) sending his subordinates to a communications course, (b) attending a communications course himself, (c) both (a) and (b), (d) trying to live with the problem, or (e) working on the problem directly. He chose the last alternative. An external OD consultant and an internal consultant from the Employee Relations Division worked on the problem with the vice president in a team development session. They designed a work session to be held from 9:00 a.m. to lunch on a regular work day in the staff meeting room. Before the meeting, several memos from the vice president to the division managers were selected and prepared on a glass slide, which could then be shown on a screen via a projector. With the vice president and consultants present, all division managers considered several of the memos according to a certain procedure. After reading the memo on the screen, they were asked three questions: (a) What do you think the message says? (2) What priority would you give to the message: (a) HIGH, take care of the matter immediately, (b) MEDIUM, take care of the matter relatively soon, or (c) LOW, take care of it when I can get to it? (3) What action would you take?

After everyone responded to the three questions by writing their answers, each manager was asked to read his response to the total group. Considerable differences occurred among the managers. Later, the vice president explained what he meant the memo to say, what priority he desired, and what action he wanted. As might be expected, a number of misunderstandings were corrected and learning resulted, both learning on the vice president's part, as well as the division managers'.

An interesting side effect resulted later in time: the vice president's memos decreased in number by 40%. Also, after a year of collecting relevant data, a considerable monetary savings amounting to approximately $20,000 was realized as a result of changes in communications procedures.

---

* Source: Harvey & Boettger (1971)

Examining relationships among team members

This fourth purpose of team building concerns identifying interpersonal problems that exist among team members and working toward some resolution of these problems. A case example of this form of team building concerned the top management group of a high-technology business organization. The climate within the group was open and spontaneous, particularly in group members' discussions of ideas and technical problems. They expressed a desire to be open with one another about their feelings and interpersonal relationships, but their individual styles and the patterns of interaction among them blocked this desire. They conformed to a nonconfronting norm when it came to interpersonal issues. This norm was reinforced by the president, who was highly analytical, rational, and sensible and was greatly admired by the subordinate team members. Eventually, a subgroup within the team emerged and began to push for facing up to the team relationship issues. They suggested that an extended meeting be held so that the group members could examine their interpersonal relationships. The suggestion was agreed to by all group members and the meeting took place.

> At this meeting each individual received some feedback from all of his colleagues about his strengths and weaknesses as they perceived them . . . [and] what bothered or pleased them about his behavior. Each individual could use this feedback any way he wished—there was no requirement for change. The feedback surfaced some historic issues that had been affecting the work of the group; for example, two people who had been competing throughout their careers maintained this competition in the group. They were perceived by all the others as sometimes robbing the group of their technical resource capability on the tasks because of their interpersonal relationship. It was agreed that the group would try to draw this to their attention whenever it arose in the future. The feedback to the president by the team was accepted and generally understood by him . . . . however, the main benefit . . . . was that it freed the group to produce this kind of information in the future as needed. This became a norm of the group and was perhaps the single most significant result. (Beckhard, 1972, p. 31)

As illustrated in this case, when the purpose of team building is to work on relationships, a critical dimension of the process is interpersonal feedback. Regardless of the purpose we may be emphasizing in a team building effort, our ultimate goal is to improve the overall effectiveness of the team as a group. It is appropriate, therefore, for us to consider at this point some of the criteria for and characteristics of an effective group.

Criteria for an effective team

Douglas McGregor observed and worked with many groups, especially in a managerial context. Based on his research, his observations, and his consultation with these different groups, he listed what he considered the unique features of an effective managerial team (McGregor, 1967).

1. Understanding, mutual agreement, and identification with respect to the primary task. Team members have clarity about their ultimate purpose or mission and are committed to its accomplishment.

2. Open communications. Team members express their ideas, opinions, and feelings openly and authentically. For further discussion of authenticity, see Herman and Korenich (1977). McGregor also points out that being absolutely open, regardless of the situation, is not the criterion for effectiveness. Openness is related to the task at hand.

3. Mutual trust. Trust and openness go hand in hand, and openness is practically impossible to achieve without trust among team members. McGregor's (1967) definition of trust is worthy of quotation:

> Trust means: "I know that you will not—deliberately or accidentally, consciously or unconsciously—take unfair advantage of me." It means: "I can put my situation at the moment, my status and self-esteem in this group, our relationship, my job, my career, even my life, in your hands with complete confidence." (p. 163)

McGregor notes further that trust is a delicate aspect of relations, influenced more by actions than by words. Trust can be destroyed quickly and easily—one act can do it. Trust is a feeling influenced by needs, expectations, guilt, anxieties, and the like, and it is based on people's perceptions of others and their behavior, not on objective reality.

4. Mutual support. This feature of an effective team is characterized by the absence of hostility or indifference among members and by the presence of care, concern, and active help toward one another.

5. Management of human differences. Group creativity typically comes from an open exchange of different ideas, opinions, and intuitions, and from an active process of integrating these differences into an outcome that represents the best of the individual contributions. Research has clearly documented that the more groups uncover and deal with their differences, the higher the quality of their decisions will be (Hall 1971; Hall & Watson 1970; Hall & Williams, 1966). Managing differences successfully within a group is easier said than done, of course. The key is to maintain a balance between fostering conflict of ideas and opinions and controlling these differences.

6. Selective use of the team. Being discriminatory about when and when not to use the team in a group endeavor for consensual decision making will help ensure time efficiency and a wise use of member energy. Effective teams know when they should meet, and they know how to use their time.

I have found the following guidelines useful in deciding when to use the team for consensual decision making:

- when you do not know who has the most expertise regarding the decision to be made,
- when implementation of the decision will require several people—most, if not all, members of the team,
- when the facts are few—when judgment and opinion are required.

These guidelines are very similar to Vroom and Yetton's (1973) more elaborate and detailed decision tree for managers' use in determining how participative to be in decision making.

7. Appropriate member skills. The effective team has among its membership—not just with the leader—the variety of skills that are needed for performance of the task and for maintenance of the team as a viable group. It is absolutely necessary that there be an adequate level of technical knowledge among the team's membership for task accomplishment. Just as necessary are the skills required to elicit that knowledge and integrate the various elements of it into a decision. These skills are of two types—task and maintenance. From the earlier work of Benne and Sheats (1948) and Bales (1950), Bennis and Shepard (1961) assembled a composite, representative list of these important skills and functions (see Table 2). The more all members of the team can develop these two sets of skills, the more effective the team is likely to be.

8. Leadership. The leadership function of an effective team is managing and integrating the other seven characteristics. It is unreasonable to assume that the leader alone can set direction, be open, trust and support team members, manage individual differences, always know when to use the team as a group, and provide all the necessary task and maintenance functions. In the effective team these characteristics become the responsibility and concern of all members. The team leader's job is to see that these characteristics are first identified and then become group norms. In addition, the team leader is the prime coordinator, seeing that the various responsibilities for effective team work are shared among members and differentiated according to subtask requirements and member talent.

Prior to McGregor's list of eight features, Likert (1961) had proposed 24 "performance characteristics of the ideal highly effective group." There is considerable overlap between the two lists, but four from Likert's list are different enough to be worth mentioning.

Table 2
Bennis and Shepard's List

Task functions	Maintenance functions
Initiating activity	Encouraging
Seeking information	Gatekeeping
Seeking opinion	Standard setting
Giving information	Following
Giving opinion	Expressing group feeling
Elaborating	Testing for consensus and commitment
Summarizing	Mediating
Testing feasibility	Relieving tension
Evaluating	

1. The values and goals of the group are integrated with and express the relevant values and needs of the members. Since the group members help to shape these values and goals (analogous to McGregor's first feature), they will be committed to and satisfied with them.

2. Group members, including the leader, believe that they as a group can accomplish the impossible. This kind of expectation stretches and challenges group members and establishes the potential for growth and development. This characteristic of an effective group is reminiscent of Vaill's (1978) "high performing systems."

3. The group understands the nature and value of constructive conformity and knows when to use it and for what purposes. Likert (1961) clarifies this characteristic:

> Although it [the group] does not permit conformity to affect adversely the creative efforts of its members, it does expect conformity on mechanical and administrative matters to save the time of members and to facilitate the group's activities. The group agrees, for example, on administrative forms and procedures, and once they have been established, it expects its members to abide by them until there is good reason to change them. (p. 166)

Actually, this characteristic of Likert's helps amplify McGregor's management-of-differences feature—the process of maintaining a balance between fostering conflict and controlling it.

4. There is mutual influence among group members and especially between the members and the leader.

Likert used the word **ideal** in the preface to his list of 24 characteristics of an effective group. McGregor's list also can be labeled ideal. Striving for these characteristics may be idealistic for a team, but it is not necessarily unrealistic. Even approximating these ideals can improve teamwork. For team building purposes, having a standard for evaluating efforts toward a more effective team is critical, not only for direction but also for motivation as well.

By way of summary, we can define team building as an activity whereby members of a work group (1) begin to understand more thoroughly the nature of group dynamics and effective teamwork, particularly the interrelationship of **process** and **content**, and (2) learn to apply certain principles and skills of group process toward greater team effectiveness.

REFERENCES

Bales, R.F. (1950). *Interaction process analysis*. Reading, MA: Addison-Wesley.

Beckhard, R. (1972). Optimizing team-building efforts. *Journal of Contemporary Business, 1*(3), 23-32.

Beckhard, R., & Harris, R.T. (1977). *Organizational transitions: Managing complex change.* Reading, MA: Addison-Wesley.

Benne, K.D., & Sheats, P. (1948). Functional roles of group members. *Journal of Social Issues, 4*(2), 41-49.

Bennis, W.G., & Shepard, H.A. (1961). *Group observation.* In W.G. Bennis, K.D. Benne, & R. Chin (Eds.), *The planning of change* (pp. 743-756). New York: Holt, Rinehart & Winston.

Burke, W.W. (1982). *Organization development: Principles and practices.* Boston: Little, Brown.

Dayal, I., & Thomas, J.M. (1968). Operation KPE: Developing a new organization. *Journal of Applied Behavioral Science, 4*(4), 473-506.

Dyer, W.E. (1977). *Team building: Issues and alternatives.* Reading, MA: Addison-Wesley.

Hall, J. (1971). Decisions, decisions, decisions. *Psychology Today, 5*(6), 51-54, 86-88.

Hall, J., & Watson, W.H. (1970). The effects of a normative intervention on group decision making performance. *Human Relations, 23,* 299-317.

Hall, J., & Williams, M.S. (1966). A comparison of decision-making performances in established and ad hoc groups. *Journal of Personality and Social Psychology, 3,* 214-222.

Harrison, R. (1972). Role negotiation: A tough-minded approach to team development. In W.W. Burke & H.A. Hornstein (Eds.), *The social technology or organization development* (pp. 84-96). San Diego, CA: University Associates.

Harvey, J.B., & Boettger, C.R. (1971). Improving communication within a managerial workshop. *Journal of Applied Behavioral Science, 7*(2), 164-179.

Herman, S.W., Korenich, M. (1977). *Authentic management: A Gestalt orientation to organizations and their development.* Reading, MA: Addison-Wesley.

Huse, E.F. (1980). *Organization development and change* (Rev. ed.). St. Paul, MN: West.

Katz, D., & Kahn, R.L. (1978). *The social psychology of organizations* (2nd ed). New York: Wiley.

Likert, R. (1961). *New patterns of management.* New York: McGraw-Hill.

McGregor, D. (1967). *The professional manager.* New York: McGraw- Hill.

Plovnick, M.S., Fry, R.E., & Rubin, I.M. (1975). New developments in OD technology: Programmed team development. *Training and Development Journal, 29*(4), 19-27.

Vaill, P.B. (1978). Toward a behavioral description of high performance systems. In M.W. McCall, Jr., & M.M. Lombardo (Eds.), *Leadership: Where else can we go?* (pp. 103-125). Durham, NC: Duke University Press.

Vroom, V.H., & Yetton, P.W. (1973). *Leadership and decision making.* Pittsburgh: University of Pittsburgh Press.

Team Building Part 1.
Designing the Intervention

Thomas H. Patten, Jr.

How can an organization increase employee satisfaction while improving overall effectiveness? Team building, a highly popular organization development technique, often produces such a happy result.

Why team building? A look before the leap

By and large, managers recognize the interdependence of employees and the need for cooperation among people to accomplish work. This is one major reason for the emphasis on building strong managerial teams. But several conditions must exist before effective teams can be developed. First, the group must have a natural reason for working together that makes sense—whether in a department, an ad hoc committee or task force, or a top management team. Second, the members of the group must be mutually dependent on one another's experience, abilities, and commitment in order to fulfill mutual objectives. Third, group members must be committed to the idea that working together as a group, rather than in isolation or in opposition, leads to more effective decisions. Last, the group must be accountable as a functioning unit within a larger organizational context.

Key to the concept of the team is communication within the group. There has to be a singleness of mission and a willingness to cooperate. The mere fact of regular reporting relationships within organizational structures does not necessarily constitute a team, even if people appear to be grouped that way on the organization chart. Boxes and arrows symbolize neither the technical and interpersonal coordination nor the emotional investment—the commitment—that go into the true team. Whereas managers and their subordinates might be able to improve their overall relationships, coordination, and communication in many situations, the word **team** should be reserved for a special type or work group.

It isn't possible to create a team in every group, even when there is singleness of mission and an absolute need to cooperate. People have different motivations—some are ambitious, devious, and uncooperative, others are abrasive, self-seeking, and complacent. Some organizations contain many loners too uncomfortable and unskilled at working in groups to ever make the transition to becoming team players. Thus, team building is not a viable intervention strategy for every group. Even where it is organizationally practicable, it might not take hold with people who have certain antithetical personality traits.

Personality traits are one thing, but issues are quite another. Specific programs and joint projects, for example, can bring labor and management forces together in a mutual effort in which leaders from both sides cooperate in achieving mutual objectives despite other fundamental differences. Workshop sessions conducted by a competent neutral human resources consultant often can help these individuals listen to one another, reduce tension, and reach agreement on some areas. The basic purpose of team building, then, is to provide a means whereby groups or teams of managers can come together in a learning setting to acquire interactive skills for accomplishing tasks. The results of such successful team building activities can be classified in three categories.

- **Results specific to one or more individuals.** Most team building efforts improve the team members' understanding of the ways in which authority, control, and power affect problem solving and data gathering. Consequently, the team can begin to experiment with new alternatives.

- **Results specific to the group's operation and behavior.** Team building activities are sometimes preceded by sessions held to clarify the team's purpose and to establish workable long-term and short-term priorities and objectives.

- **Results that affect the group's relationships with the rest of the organization.** As the team members examine their own operation, studying communication and problem-solving techniques applicable to their own interpersonal processes, they come to see the big picture and to clarify their roles within the organization as a whole. Thus a successful team building effort can go beyond the group; it can facilitate role negotiation between team members and "interfacing" organizational units, opening the door to possibilities of cross-functional communication within the organization.

Analysis of two case studies of team building will illustrate the theoretical concepts. The common denominator in both cases is the goal of knitting together a group of people sharing task responsibilities in a tense sociotechnical situation. The team building models employed involved sustained efforts, the first effort having extended over a period of five years in 30 separate one-week workshops, and the second case being an ongoing effort of more than two years that shows promise and will probably receive managerial support for at least another year.

The Fedmil study: Federal civil service and military managers

The first of the two case studies is called Fedmil, signifying that it involves federal civil service managers and military managers (U.S. Army officers) holding key positions in a major military command that operates throughout the world. The specific tasks of Fedmil need not concern us especially, although it is worth noting that Fedmil is not a line organization, such as the infantry or the artillery, but is composed largely of highly educated engineering, electronic, scientific, and support personnel. The mix of specialisms predominant among managers in Fedmil is not unlike those found at AT&T, RCA, Raytheon, Honeywell, or IBM. Indeed, many Fedmil people had prior work experience in these organizations.

The participants in the Fedmil team building effort were high-ranking civilian managers (modal grade: GS-14) and military managers (modal rank: lieutenant colonel).

The need for the series of team building workshops had previously been established by data gathered on relationships among the following three classes of managers at Fedmil: managers who were civilians, but not retired military personnel; managers who were civilians, but were also retired officers; and managers who were Army officers on active duty. The need was determined by observation, reports from top management, and a fiat and mandate from the top, rather than by the use of such empirical tools as questionnaires and interviews.

Frequently, noncombat units in military organizations are headed by a military officer whose immediate subordinate is a civilian. This one-over-one relationship (in a sense, two persons for one job), is based on the fact that the officer is subject to rotation every three years. The civilian subordinate remains to provide continuity in the direction of the organization's activity. Often the activity is technical or highly specialized, necessitating increased reliance on the civilian subordinate, at least when a high-ranking officer has been newly assigned to the job. Even so, the top job in the activity is typically reserved for a military officer, and a civilian cannot aspire to it. That many civilians are retired officers exacerbates the problem, as they may consider themselves more knowledgeable than the mobile officers on active duty or the younger, mobile career civil servants. When collaboration among these three types of managerial employee is impaired, an organization development (OD) intervention is warranted. In such circumstances, team building, perhaps in the form of a small-group training experience conducted by an outside consultant, often has substantial promise.

In this case, the different organizational components nominated the executives who would participate in the team building effort. Most attendees were white men, 35 to 55 years of age. Very few minority group members or women attended, because at the time the OD seminars/workshops were offered, few such individuals had become upwardly mobile enough to reach the high-ranking military and executive levels the program was designed to assist.

The seminars/workshops were called Organization Development Through Team Building (ODTTB). The program was initially conceived as a special set of interrelated seminars and workshops designed to aid Fedmil management in developing its team skills, ability to plan and control work, and competence in motivating subordinates. The program was designed to educate or develop top executives for team building. Participants were those who could be given time off the job and who were willing to attend. The major sessions of the team building workshops and seminars are exhibited in Table 1.

Built around a theoretical model and strategy for organizational change, ODTTB made use of both originally developed and commercially available material. It involves pulling the right levers in a strategy for change, which can be depicted linearly (see Figure 1).

The basic premise of the strategy is that in order to change executive behavior, the executives' awareness of their personal managerial styles must be raised to the point where they want to develop and improve the management of their organization. They are provided with an opportunity to learn skills as team members in reaching decisions based on consensus and resolution of interpersonal conflict. Next, the workshop provides them with practice in goal setting, work planning and review, problem solving, and time management—all basic to MBO. The final step in the process ties application of their new skills in with the organization's reward system. Working with the MBO processes in which they have been trained, and using their new interpersonal skills, managers can relate to employees and reward them, both financially and nonfinancially, to motivate them to perform assigned work to high standards. The Lewinian notion of unfreezing, changing, and refreezing is implicit in the seminar/workshop design. The goals of the team building seminar/workshops were as follows:

- to help participants establish a sense of teamwork and mutual trust in their respective organizational components;

Table 1

Design of the Team Building Seminar/Workshop

Time	MONDAY: Self-awareness as a manager	TUESDAY: Group decision making and consensus building	WEDNESDAY: MBO and problem solving	THURSDAY: MBO, interpersonal communication issues, and delegation skills	FRIDAY: OD, MBO, and reward administration
8:30-12:00	Theory input on OD	Theory input on team building	Theory input on MBO	Theory input on rational and emotional issues in MBO problem solving	Theory input on OD, MBO, and rewards and penalties
	Johari Window	Desert survival problem	MBO exercise on regular objectives	MBO exercise on innovative goals	MANDOERS* exercise on development and rewards
	FIRO-B exercise; form teams	Debriefing and relating exercise to job	Debriefing of exercise	Debriefing of exercise	Debriefing of exercise
12:00-1:00	Lunch	Lunch	Lunch	Lunch	Lunch
1:00-3:30	Theory input on behavioral science	Theory input on consensus	Theory input problem solving and innovative MBO	Theory input on the management of managerial time	Theory input on the helping relationship in management and feedback
	Managerial style	Interpersonal conflict management exercise	MBO exercise on problem-solving goals	Time management and delegation exercise	Team peer evaluations
	System intervention exercise				
	Debriefing of exercise	Debriefing of exercise	Debriefing of exercise	Debriefing of exercise	Debriefing of exercise
	Unfreezing		Changing		Refreezing

*MANDOERS is an acronym for management development, organizational effectiveness, and reward system.

Figure 1. Strategy for change.

- to enable participants to develop skills in resolving conflicts with persons and groups, communicating openly with others, confronting issues, and conducting interpersonal relations with peers, subordinates, counterparts, and superiors;
- to assist participants in understanding how to motivate others and promote dedication to getting the job done;
- to review and examine basic managerial skills in such areas as work planning, setting managerial objectives, controlling activities so that goals are attained, managing the use of time, solving problems, and getting employees on the team;
- to connect ideas about manager and employee behavior and motivation with the administration of salaries and nonfinancial rewards.

The program was designed to implement these goals and to provide flexibility for the addition of modules at a later date, if desired, or for teams requiring further work in, for example, MBO, role negotiation, time management, and career life planning. Thus the design of the program was sufficiently structured to permit learning, but flexible enough to allow for any other necessary OD interventions.

Participants in the ODTTB seminars/workshops were given the option to work in teams that included the boss and subordinates either in a direct line relationship or in a functional staff relationship. Thus, there were several cases in which the teams fit the team building requisite of a natural, intact group, but most were artificial, composed of high-level managers who split their time between working together closely and working apart from the group.

If we step back from ODTTB, we are able to examine the difference between team building itself and an executive seminar/workshop on team building. The latter is concerned with learning about learning, while the former is used to translate the learning into action on the job. Learning about learning—the phenomenon of adults coming to realize that they are responsible for their own growth and can best learn many complex skills by working together on developmental tasks—has always been one of the primary goals of the T Group in laboratory training. Yet the findings demonstrate that team building seminars/workshops can also provide an opportunity for learning about learning. For the most part, however, team building used in organizations for group development appears to center on creating an awareness of the realities of unequal power accountability and the participants' relationships to the larger system rather than on personal growth per se.

An interesting contrast to the Fedmil team building study is the Basmanco model, the second of the two studies.

The Basmanco study: Basic manufacturing company

The Basmanco team building study is part of a continuing effort at a basic manufacturing plan in one division of a **Fortune** 500 firm. The data pertain to 35 participants, representing 10% of a total population of 350 employees. The mix consists of the plant manager, all managers reporting directly to him, and about 25 unionized office employees supervised by the plant manager's managerial subordinates.

Rooted in an action research methodology, the Basmanco study is governed by the $OD_1 \rightarrow MBO \rightarrow RS$ theoretical stance described for Fedmil. The sequence of steps carried out at Basmanco is summarized in Table 2. This OD effort was slowly implemented over two years, and several interventions are projected for the future. The ability of Basmanco to absorb the OD interventions and move toward behavioral and organizational change governed the tempo of the implementation effort.

Figure 2 portrays the nature of the interrelationships among the management consultant, or external change agent; the plant personnel manager, or internal change agent; and the client, who was the plant manager. The interrelationships shown are typical of many OD change efforts in the United States, whether they are used for team building or for other purposes. The double arrows in the triad suggest that all three principals in the change effort will continue to communicate and trust one another over time.

Returning to the Basmanco team building effort described in Table 2, we see that the change activity has evolved around off-site meetings, as opposed to the laboratory setting of seminars/workshops. The meetings dealt with live organizational problems and appear to be as close as we can come to the real-life, on-the-job situation. This setting is less conducive to learning about learning than to a desire to solve problems that will have an impact on the way in which employees and managers interact.

The activities presented in Table 2 were supplemented by the plant personnel manager's intercession. Committees set up by action planning met during the workday several times monthly. These task forces zeroed in on the problem areas and proposed solutions for implementation that

Table 2

Basmanco Action Research Chronology

Date	Activity and purpose	Result
August 1976	Two days of diagnostic interviewing and data gathering to identify problems and issues	Formulation of report to be used for off-site meeting
September 1976	One-day off-site meeting, attendance of 35, to react to data and plan preliminary actions	Establishment of four labor-management committees (informal task forces or teams) focused on • trust and communication in management • trust and communication in union • discipline • grievance procedure
January 1977	One-day off-site meeting similar to September meeting	Report of committees and redesignation of committees to • efficiency committee working on problems of a new management information systems (MIS) • union committee • labor education committee • grievance committee
May 1977	Similar to the January 1977 effort	Reduction of four committees to one interdepartmental committee to deal with MIS
September 1977	One-day meeting with plant manager and personnel manager to check progress and plant department managers to plan union and lower-level plan department managers	Diagnostic interviewing and beginning of extension of OD to the plan
September 1977	Presentation of OD effort to divisional VP and other executives	Obtained corporate expression of interest
October 1977	One-day off-site meeting for 12 key managers only (office and plant)	Informed of corporate meeting, reviewed motivation theory, and revealed styles and aspirations

did not conflict with any provisions of the collective bargaining agreement. This was to avoid any allegation that an OD intervention was being used to undermine the union or to organize for union busting. Indeed, our goal was the opposite: to help the union develop more solidarity, to unify labor-management relations, and to give union members insights into union structure, philosophy, and dynamics.

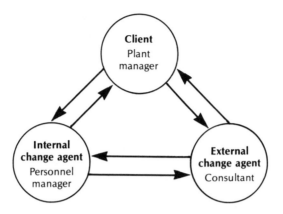

The in-house manager's side	What the consultant brings
• Knowledge of specific sociotechnical systems	• Knowledge of OD techniques
• Perspective limited to organization (local outlook)	• Experience in many organizations, variety of perspectives (cosmopolitan outlook)
• Dependency on organization for financial rewards	• Independence
• Company-person career bond	• No bond; easily dispensable relationship

Figure 2. The OD change-effort triad.

In essence, the task approximated trying to catch a bucket of smoke. The problem as identified by the plant manager and personnel manager was an insidious atmosphere of interpersonal animosities; deep-rooted hard feelings of employees, in some cases going back a decade or more; leadership rivalry in the virtually all-female office union; and managerial chicanery and game playing in the grievance procedure.

There were several other complicating factors as well. The office was about 75 years old, dirty, poorly maintained, hot in the summer, cold in the winter, and physically unattractive. The office had once been a divisional headquarters, but the location had been downgraded to plant status within a larger division, with many employees unable or unwilling to accept the real consequences of the loss in status, and behaving as if it had never happened.

Most of the employees had at least ten years' service; some had been on the job 30 to 40 years. Nothing had ever been done before to deal with the physical and interpersonal office problems. Petty jealousy and resentments had simmered interminably. No one ostensibly wanted change, and yet when interviewed on an individual basis, many employees expressed feelings of hurt and pain.

Determined to try something to improve the climate, the plant manager had hired a well-qualified young personnel manager to analyze what was going on and what might be done about it. Several older, long-service key managers felt the climate was satisfactory as it existed, but some of the new managers considered the office the worst they had ever worked in from the standpoint of interpersonal relations. Many cross-currents of feelings had to be dealt with.

Other facets of the social situation at Basmanco needed to be worked out as well—the recognizable isolated ethnic groups among unionized employees and managers, and the fact that personnel managers had typically lasted only a short time and then quit.

The plant was highly profitable and had been for several years. The plant manager was extremely capable, well respected, and clearly committed to leading the change effort from the top and persevering with it—as solid and well supported a commitment as an external change agent could expect.

The image of the bucket of smoke disbands in the face of the positive, ongoing team building program that was instituted at Basmanco. It is scheduled to proceed into the future.

Team Building Part 2. Conducting the Intervention

Thomas H. Patten, Jr.

The first installment of Dr. Patten's discussion of team building interventions analyzed two case studies, one called Fedmil (federal civil service and military managers) and one called Basmanco (basic manufacturing company), both of which were successful. In Part 2 of this study, Dr. Patten compares the diagnoses, interventions, and results of both team building models

The methods of diagnosis, types of interventions, and results attained at Fedmil—a military operation—and Basmanco—a **Fortune** 500 basic manufacturing company—are identified and compared in Table 1. The comparison is striking when we consider the diagnostic techniques, organization size, types of interventions, background of the internal change agents, target groups in the team building endeavor, results (showing mostly "soft," nonquantitative data, except for the "hard" data on Basmanco grievances, which were resolved to the mutual satisfaction of the parties), and financing (not often discussed in the OD literature as an important facet of OD studies, but perhaps the best measure of determining whether the effort is merely an under-financed shoestring wish of a zealous and intellectually curious staff person or an amply budgeted endeavor openly supported by top management and the chief financial authority in the work organization). An additional item of hard data pertinent to Basmanco is that for the first time in six years of contract negotiations an agreement was reached in 1978 without a strike.

Table

Comparison of Diagnoses, Interventions, and Results

Factors	Fedmil	Basmanco
Diagnosis	Need determination by fiat based on observation and judgment of internal change agent	Data gathered through interviewing of a sample of 20 employees by external change agent
Employee size	30,000 (but fewer than 1,000 in top management)	350
Types of interventions	Not top led—top executive and executives superficially aware of effort (and some probably not aware at all); seminars/workshops tailor made by a mixture of cognitive and experienced exercises	Top led. Top executive actively involved and committed. Off-site semistructured feedback and action-planning sessions; limited cognitive input in seminars
Character of internal change agents	Internal change agent supportive of consulting and having knowledge of OD (formal title: staff employee development specialist)	Internal change agent supportive of consulting with more limited knowledge of OD (formal title: personnel manager)
Target groups in team building	Managers and primary staff action officers (PSADs)	Managers and office union members
Results	Reported increases in self- and team awareness and movement toward a more healthy organization	Resolution of 17 formal grievances (some going back three years); greater insight and knowledge of labor union philosophy and operations by unionized employees
	More leveling on performance appraisals	Some reduction of inter-personal bickering, backbiting, and pettiness
	Exposure to MBO, time management, and reward system administration and some applications of each by managers and PSADs	Exposure to office and plant functions and products and to cross-departmental problems
	Greater use of consensual approaches in managing	Greater insight into management's perspective and problems
Financing	Ample and justified comptrollers likely to continue	Ample and justified to comptroller; likely to continue

Analysis of Fedmil and Basmanco—the concept of the OD stance

In the role of external change agent, I have felt a need over the years to provide a rationale for studying what I am doing when I intervene and where I am in sociotechnical and social psychological space, so to speak, after working on OD with a client system. In 1972 I first set forth the OD-MBO-R stance (see Figure 1). It is now a check point and orientation to my OD work as it progresses. This notion can be expanded and related to the team building work at Fedmil and Basmanco.

A stance should not be regarded as either a canned approach or the consultant's proverbial standard solution looking for a problem, but rather as a diagnostic starting point for beginning OD work once initial contact has been made with a client and the external change agent's thinking processes have started. One needn't be rigid in her or his stance, but there are likely to be predilections or, more grossly, biases in the change agent that condition how he or she proceeds in applying certain interventions. Even the relatively structureless stance would reflect the stance of the external change agent in order to facilitate working on a particular problem or issue. We can deny that we have stances, but if we do, I think we are engaging in self-deception.

How does the OD-MBO-R stance help me in working with Fedmil and Basmanco? The initial diagnosis of the problems at Fedmil was provided by the internal change agent, who has lived with the particular system for several years and had almost 30 years' experience in similar organizations. He essentially judged the manifest and latent problems that were presumably impairing the functioning of the organization and placed an "order" with the external change agent in much the same way that a person would drive to a gas station and direct the attendant to fill the tank with regular, high-test, or lead-free gasoline. We might say that if the attendant has the necessary and sufficient skills for pumping gas, the order can be filled with alacrity.

Similarly, if the external change agent has the requisite skills, he or she should be able to fill the client's OD needs. But the analogy falls apart because the professional ideology and outlook of external change agents causes them to question the "order" in terms of its diagnostic propriety and accuracy, the receptivity of the client system to change, the extent to which important power wielders in the organization share

Organization development ⟶ management by objectives ⟶ rewards

(OD) (MBO) (R)

Figure 1. Strategy for change

the inside change agent's diagnosis, and many other factors. Unless the external change agent is blind (which may mean stanceless in this context), he would probably immediately think of his values and the configuration of variables that comprise his stance. This thinking process would trigger off the rush of all kinds of reservations about proceeding on an order-placing basis. Need must govern the direction of OD. How does one reconcile need with an "order"?

The initial entry at Fedmil was a hypothetical realization that I would probably be working on behavioral issues with great intensity, but that this probably would not be sufficient because problems in goal setting, gaining the commitment of subordinate employees to perform (my interpretation of motivation), the management of time, and coping with a management-by-crisis ambience were also problems. Thus I sensed that I would need to think of an unfreezing stage that would involve some social-emotional unblocking and the introduction of some rational tools of management. I had a prior awareness of the relative rigidities of the military and federal financial compensation systems, which suggested that if there were problems with the reward system, they may have gone underground or been thought to be unsolvable because of systemic rigidities.

More broadly, Fedmil was clearly an organizational component in a larger bureaucracy (the Department of the Army), a subset of a larger system (the Department of Defense), which was, lastly, part of a still larger supersystem, the U.S. government. This bureaucratic layering could be expected to provide a proverbial "they" for Fedmil to be concerned with, which would probably set the parameters for the autonomy and fiscal, personal, and policy integrity of Fedmil.

All this thinking provided a basis for meaningful conjecture on how to design interventions and engage in the OD latching-on process. In brief, I considered that I would probably be best off designing around self-awareness and group-awareness issues, while assessing where some of the deficiencies were in work-performance motivation and existing management systems. As a matter of fact, this is exactly where my design work ultimately took me, except that I became more heavily involved in explaining a planning and control concept of MBO and providing skills in how to implement it than I had anticipated. The reward system proved impervious to change in major ways and a weak tool for use in reinforcing MBO in Fedmil. Changes in the reward system would have to be made by higher management for Fedmil executives to believe it was intended to be a more credible lever for employee performance change. As a result, I see myself presently involved in considerable basic team building and helping in MBO and development of time-management skills. In one location in Fedmil I have introduced modular two-day seminars/workshops in career and life planning and time management and delegation, based again on the perceived need judged by an employee-development specialist.

The large-scale midcareer shifting of Army officers to civilian life through retirement in addition to the introspection engaged in these days by many upper middle managers have indicated that career- and life-planning interventions would be helpful for the person and essentially beneficial to obtaining career commitment from key employees. Time management and delegation skills seem to be required to work in a fast-moving environment where the federal government is controlling head counts, attempting to reduce average salary grade levels, and seeking simultaneously (and perhaps inconsistently) to increase productivity. Getting more with less is a current Fedmil managerial drive. It is also increasing heartburn among executives and generating a still greater need for OD. In fact, the Army has begun to institutionalize OD (calling it OE—organizational effectiveness) in an effort to manage itself better in our present environment of perilous budgets and presidential desires to reduce the size of the federal work force.

Turning to Basmanco, the OD-MBO-R stance enabled me to check out where to begin the interventions. Basmanco has had an MBO system for many years that it regards as quite satisfactory for managerial employees. Managers and employees consider wages and salaries to be excellent. The collective bargaining agreement is, of course, very explicit on wages, hours, and working conditions. Thus, it did not seem fruitful to design initial OD interventions at Basmanco in these areas compared to interventions that would help improve the patterns of interpersonal relations in the office. The sustained profitability of the plant and the virtual absence of any discussion of pay and its administration would perplex the student of management or ardent trade unionist. Their stance is to see problems in work organizations in largely economic terms and to minimize the significance of problems in the sociotechnical system when the economic indices are positive.

Summary

The OD stance in operation at Fedmil and Basmanco is helpful in diagnosing and designing interventions and thinking about measuring the results of the interventions. Having a well-thought-out stance points to where contributions can be made as the OD effort unfolds over time. Equally important, the OD stance sets the boundaries of the effort; it avoids areas where a consultant might have little or no expertise and signals the need for the internal change agent to call on another consultant for guidance in continuing OD work in areas where this would be the best course of action.

Conclusions

The OD-MBO-R model is widely adaptable, as evidenced by its application at Fedmil and Basmanco, two organizations of vastly different size and scope. It provides a cognitive map that enables the external change agent to work from a versatile stance and "strategize" what needs to be done to bring about change in an overall, sustained team building effort. The questions are: Can team building be regarded as a unitary OD phenomenon in any sense? Is there any value in considering two such disparate OD efforts as Fedmil and Basmanco?

In both cases, the groups working through the two different team building designs for the purpose of improving the management of their organizations have had a reason or economic **raison d'etre** to do so—they **must** work together. The members of the groups in both cases are interdependent in the job and task structures. They need to "interface" acceptably to arrive at mutual goals. They are in the process of becoming committed to the idea that working together in intermeshing groups, rather than laboring egocentrically as isolated entities, leads to more effective decisions, even though Fedmil is a superlarge system in a still larger set of systems.

Finally, the employees involved in the team building effort are accountable to higher management, but not as autonomously functioning groups. I have treated them as synthetic teams, rather than as intact superior/subordinate sets, except for instances where they were intact sets. Even at Basmanco, the management-union team may be viewed as synthesized, although perhaps an effective contrary argument could probably be marshalled. We are, however, working on team skills in a broader sense. It is not the normal reporting relationship that provides the social comment for the teams at Fedmil and Basmanco, but rather the realization that managers, action officers, and unionized employees interface in carrying out complex work—they must mesh if the ultimate organizational mission is to be fulfilled and the intermediate objectives of lower levels of management are to be met.

I am seeking, in both cases, to create an awareness of the need for a profound, personal emotional investment in the team and the work itself for all individuals working in the two organizations. While the personality makeup of some people makes it difficult for them to work in a consensus mode and be "on the team," all should attempt to extend themselves to one another and adopt an open, authentic, problem-solving interpersonal style.

The data for the Fedmil and Basmanco team building efforts suggest definite improvement in team functioning and newly acquired team skills. The input of MBO theory at Fedmil has helped clarify organizational purpose for managers and action officers and has brought about a greater sense of clarity and direction in their work. However, still greater clarity and consistency could be attained if higher echelons were to improve the way in which they set and communicate goals and priorities. Nothing has been done with respect to MBO at Basmanco, but probably nothing is perceived as needed.

Finally, those who have acquired team skills as a consequence of participation in the Fedmil and Basmanco OD efforts may not have acted like behavioral science "Typhoid Marys," but there is a noticeably improved interpersonal climate at both Fedmil and Basmanco. To be sure, a great deal of work remains to be done at Fedmil because of the vast size and far-flung scope of the organization. In fact, Fedmil is not doing enough team building fast enough. Large organizations experiencing rapid turnover, mobility, and continuous organizational change require accelerated and massive injections of change agentry, probably far more than can be provided by one external change agent and a few internal change agents. A lack of speed may mean failure of the overall change effort and reflect the phenomenon of running fast merely to keep up. In contrast, Basmanco seems to be experiencing properly paced change and interventions because of its relatively small size and capacity for absorption, practice, and implementation of newly acquired team skills by managers and employees.

The bottom line

Team building is broader than action research and inclusive of many widely disparate methods of OD diagnosis and types of intervention designs. How do we know when we have arrived at the stage of the built team? What is needed is some relevant criteria for a built team. The OD-MBO-R stance might be used to devise a means of pinpointing relevant indicators. But at our present stage of conceptualizing team building in work organizations, it might be wise to think of the built team as encompassing almost any group of individuals whose social emotional bonds were tightened and whose technical or managerial skills were sharpened in order to fulfill individual and organizational purposes. Accordingly, the two team building efforts at Fedmil and Basmanco are presently evolving toward the state of the built team.

Section II.
Theory and Dynamics

Team Work: Building Productive Relationships

Marvin R. Weisbord

Teamwork is the quintessential contradiction of a society grounded in individual achievement. Without teamwork, we cannot fully experience productive community. Everybody "knows" this; rugged individualists generally like watching football or basketball—exquisite exercises in cooperation and competition—better than anything else. "Management team" ranks with "quality" as a business cliché, and the term denotes a group of persons and their common boss. On rare occasions, a management team might produce teamwork spontaneously, like kids in a schoolyard at recess. As do any professionals, most management teams learn because they need and want to. This requires observing themselves at work and unlearning deeply ingrained, self-limiting assumptions about individual effort and authority that work **against** cooperation.

One way to unlearn bad habits is through "team building," a versatile tool for improving the skills required by a productive community. Contrary to popular wisdom, team building does **not** simply mean well-run meetings in which people "stick to the agenda." Instead, team building strives for effective meetings with agenda addressing both tasks and processes.

The team building format evolved in the early 1960s as one solution to the dilemma of "transferring training," or using laboratory learning in "real life." This dilemma still plagues training specialists, who universally agree—with Frederick Taylor and Douglas McGregor—that the greater the integration of learning and doing, the better one can achieve both. The following two insights emerged from efforts to merge T Group learning with organizational life.

1. People who belonged to "stranger" groups often had powerful "ah-ha" experiences of revelation or inspiration, which they could not describe to their coworkers or translate into new organizational policies, structures, systems, or procedures.
2. When trainers sought to remedy this situation by running T Groups **within** organizations, they found that people dredged up emotional issues too remote from the tasks at hand to be dealt with properly through that format.

The learning itself, however—especially the capability to distinguish between task and process, what and how, things and feelings, ends and means—was important for improving productivity and satisfaction in one's work. In T Groups people learned to trust one another and to accept and synthesize their differences. A way had to be found to make this learning legitimate and accessible in the work place. This called for leadership, the identification of mutual goals, control of the decision to proceed by those whose relationships were to be improved, and "task structures" different from—but not alien to—"organizational reality."

Some wariness is appropriate. Team building has come to represent everything from interpersonal encounters among coworkers (a format I do not recommend) to joint work on tasks of mutual importance (a format I strongly support). The most powerful team building occurs when people rethink together an organization's future potential, its central tasks, and the design of jobs, policies, and systems so that pursuing the future and tasks will be more enjoyable for each organization member.

Many methods

A great variety of solutions evolved using consultants, workbooks, cassette tapes, facilitators, and more. Of many "OD" techniques, the team meeting has proven durable, flexible, and useful for a wide range of situations, including starting new teams and task forces, reorganizing, untangling conflicts among departments, cooperating in setting goals, planning strategy, and managing cultural change—in short, any activity people cannot do alone. Well-motivated groups can now routinely learn how to manage themselves and their work with less frustration and more productivity.

I emphasize the term "well-motivated," because motivation is the building block for all constructive change. A team cannot play winning football if half of its members do not give a damn. The same is true for producing, selling, or managing anything. This does require work; even the best-intentioned groups must "flounder" for a day or two the first time they endeavor to hold a team building meeting. One cannot get to renewal without first passing through confusion. Afterwards, maintaining renewal requires perhaps two meetings a year, with the agenda including team processes. This becomes more important if, as is common, team composition changes.

Team building "works" when the following four conditions are met:

1. **Interdependence.** The team is working on important problems in which each person has a stake. That is, teamwork is central to success, not merely an expression of ideology or some misplaced "ought-to."
2. **Leadership.** The boss wants so strongly to improve group performance that he or she will take risks.
3. **Joint decision.** All members agree to participate.
4. **Equal influence.** Each person has a chance to influence the agenda.

In one typical scenario, the boss calls a meeting, states some personal goals, and calls for discussion. When, as is common, a consultant has been asked to help, the parties need a "get-acquainted" meeting. Often, the consultant interviews team members to discover their concerns and wishes. Questions might include those designed to uncover each person's objectives, tasks, problems, and the extent of help needed from others.

The consultant presents a summary of interview themes to the team, inviting discussion of the pros and cons of continuing. If the team decides to proceed, it schedules a two- or three-day off-site event. This meeting has a dual focus that makes it different from typical staff meetings. The team works directly on an important task identified by the members, such as strategy formation; reorganizing; dealing with technology, costs, or markets; quality; or customer problems. Team members also specify what they wish to improve in their own processes. This enables them to step back periodically and observe what they are doing to help or hinder progress. To help this discussion, process-analysis forms such as the one presented in Table 1 can be used.

Such forms are easily constructed. One can spend days in a library researching the issues that decades of research have indicated accompany productivity and satisfaction. Or one can ask the team members which issues are important—and obtain roughly the same list in 10 minutes.

Making such a list is a focusing exercise, a learning tool. Done once or twice, it helps people internalize key processes. Done by rote, however, it becomes a meaningless ritual, analogous to producing reams of numbers in a quarterly report that nobody pays attention to.

A more powerful way to help people understand their own processes is to videotape a meeting. Reviewing ten minutes of the tape and asking participants to recall what they thought or felt during that period is probably the simplest way to facilitate team learning. Sports teams,

Table 1						
Rating Team Development						

Where do you see our team right now? (circle rating)

1. Team's purpose						
I'm uncertain	1	2	3	4	5	I'm clear
2. Membership						
I'm out	1	2	3	4	5	I'm in
3. Elbow room						
I'm crowded	1	2	3	4	5	I'm comfortable
4. Discussion						
Cautious/guarded	1	2	3	4	5	Open/free
5. Use of skills						
Poor	1	2	3	4	5	Full
6. Support						
For self only	1	2	3	4	5	For all members
7. Conflict						
Avoided	1	2	3	4	5	Worked on
8. Influence on decisions						
By few members	1	2	3	4	5	By all members

tennis players, and other athletes often learn by watching tapes of their performances.

The dual focus on both task **and** process is the team building meeting's unique contribution to productive community. I find three criteria for success in this.

1. The team must resolve important dilemmas, often ones on which little progress was made before.
2. Members must emerge from the meeting more confident of their ability to influence the future.
3. Members must learn how much productivity is linked to their own candor, responsibility for themselves, and willingness to cooperate with others.

Practical theory

I want to describe the underlying theory of team building in business terms, borrowing from the work of the late Mike Blansfield, who pioneered the method years ago in working with TRW and other companies. He called his core concept "team effectiveness theory." Figure 1 provides a model of this. Blansfield's theory can be used with all sorts of procedures, and highlights factors that people in business rarely associate with results. Most managers do not define output in terms of teamwork but instead describe positive results with a vocabulary including

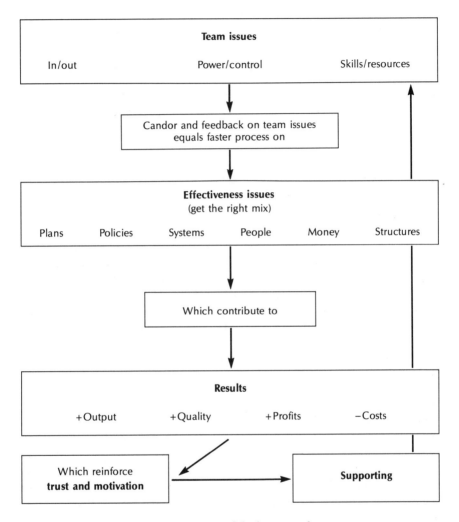

Figure 1. A model of teamwork

higher productivity, better quality, increased profits, and lower costs, as indicated in Figure 1.

When something in the list at the bottom of this flow chart goes wrong, managers feel out of control and (secretly) incompetent. They initiate searches for mistakes in techniques, policies, systems, and plans (the middle of the chart) or try to blame a villain. In extreme cases, they fire persons.

Few managers consider the impact of their own behavior on the **key processes** affected by the situation. These processes are presented at the top of the chart. Researchers from Taylor to Lewin to McGregor have identified managers' own behavior as the best starting point for improving systems, labor-management relations, productivity, satisfaction with work, company culture—or anything else. Blansfield's model highlights the difference between managing a problem "one on one" and managing a group of persons depending on one another. Doing the latter requires one to appreciate both tasks and processes and how they apply to management teamwork.

Adding teamwork to effectiveness

I quickly learned to appreciate Blansfield's model because of my own management experiences years ago. About 1960, in the days of the 80-column punch card and key verifier (remember them, senior citizens?), I installed a computerized order processing system in a firm I was managing. Systems analysts from outside the company told us what we needed. Programmers instructed the computer to do the work. The rest of us waited expectantly for results. I never considered that this new technology would change everybody's job—including my own—reduce personal control over customer policy, and force us to rethink many nonroutine problems. I had never seen a computer before; hardly anybody had. In the days before "user friendliness," I had an aggravating initiation.

I vividly recall the disruption, missed deadlines, angry customers, tearful order-processing clerks, bewildered systems analysts, and general turmoil that resulted in two resignations and the loss of several customers. Who knows what our collective blood pressure measurements were, how many of us got ulcers, how many smoke or drank more heavily? I fell prey to a common tendency of task-driven managers: When things began to go wrong, I worked harder and faster at what I knew best. I pressured people to work overtime, I chided the office force for not cooperating. I repeated my goals for rapid implementation. I made changes in the system, rerouting Form A from Desk B to Desk C and having a carbon copy sent to Person D. I checked to make certain the copy went to the accounting department. In short, I worked hard on the effectiveness factors, as if feelings and motivation had nothing to do with the situation. Managing one on one with a driving force, I drove everybody nuts—including myself.

My motor had a missing cylinder. I thought I was managing computer systems technology and acted as if each person were a cog in the machine. I triggered a set of social dynamics about which I knew nothing—the factors listed at the top of Blansfield's model. Each person in a work group continually struggles with three questions that are never answered "once and for all," but must continually be resolved at every turning point.

1. Am I in or out?
2. Do I have any power and control?
3. Can I use, develop, and be appreciated for my skills and resources?

In or out. Most of us want to belong, to be valued, to have tasks that matter, and to be recognized by others as insiders. The more "in" we feel, the better we cooperate; the more "out" we feel, the more we withdraw, work alone, daydream, and defeat ourselves and others. When I sought single handedly to patch up the computer system, I drove everybody else "out."

Power and control. Everybody wants power. When faced with changes we cannot influence, we feel impotent and come to lose self-esteem—regardless of how smart one is, how skillful, how successful. When something arises that one cannot handle, one may work harder and do worse, until one gains control again. That happened to me during the computerization, and I made things worse for everyone.

Skills and resources. Tremendous amounts of skill, experience, and common sense exist in every work place. Preventing us from tapping them are outdated assumptions about who can or should do what. Often, jobs become defined so narrowly that people cannot use their brains or even the training they have received. During my firm's computer installation, I considered people's years of experience with the old system to be irrelevant. I pressured them to change abruptly their ways of doing things and learn something no one had any experience with. Lacking a team concept, I saw no way of helping persons support one another as they learned. In short, I was not only managing a computer installation—but also the destruction of a social system of trust, motivation, and commitment that had been built over many years. The simple truth is that all the interdependent changes being made meant that the systemic change could **not** be managed successfully one on one. The three team process issues can only be resolved when the tasks are seen as team tasks, not as a problem the boss must solve. In addition, the issues will not be resolved unless two things occur: Members must learn how to state openly what is on their minds, and they must be responsive to others. They must give and receive feedback.

Candor and feedback. Candor and feedback link team issues with results. People need a place where they can discuss what each person needs to do and one's anxiety about doing it. We need the chance to admit to feeling uncertain and express differences of opinion constructively. We need to discover that others feel as we do. We need one thing more as well. I have been involved in dozens of team meetings, and eventually someone **always** brings up the importance of trust. Commitment is built on a foundation of mutual trust, and everybody knows it. Trusting one another provides the most secure way of managing through tough times. The team building meeting provides one way for persons to learn how to develop trust.

Feelings about membership, control, and skills influence one's motivation, which in turn determines the quality of one's work. If we talk **only** about results, tasks, and plans—without determining how well we can listen and hear, discuss differences, solve problems, and make decisions in ways that foster commitment—we ultimately defeat the results we claim to value. It is all one system. Pull on any one thread, and you untangle the whole net—the task of a dual-focus meeting.

Structure. A team building meeting is helped by structure. Usually a team building meeting starts with a discussion of goals and agenda. Often, considerable discussion is required just to get consensus about the major agenda—the why, how, what, and who. Sometimes prearranged "stop action" points occur in which team members complete process observation forms or review a videotape. Sometimes a consultant will call for a "time out" if persons are fighting or avoiding a task. Usually, a short discussion of process is sufficient to put the meeting back on track. This may take several hours of discussion. In any event, the team's own process requirements should remain in focus.

If persons identify interpersonal conflicts or difficulty in communicating as sources of frustration, a personal style instrument—such as a self-report survey using paper and pencil—may trigger a half-day discussion. In such an exercise, persons learn to value their differences, accept their strengths, and express themselves more clearly.

Sometimes teams engage in role negotiation, a procedure devised by consultant Roger Harrison (1971). Each team member writes down what he or she wants each of the others to do less of, more of, or the same. These requests are then posted and negotiated. For example, one person may offer, "I'll give you at least a week's notice of schedule changes if you'll refer customer complaints directly to me." No deal is made unless both parties agree.

Responsibility charting, another useful technique, is indicated if the team's self-diagnosis is that important tasks are "falling through the cracks." Figure 2 presents a responsibility chart on which the team lists who makes which decisions, who must be informed of them, who must support them, and who has the power to veto them (Galbraith, 1977). All these activities increase communication, provide feedback, consider each person's needs, distribute influence more equitably, and promote orderly procedures for managing interdependence.

Leadership and consensus. Nearly every team eventually addresses how the boss makes decisions—the authority-dependency issue. Inevita-

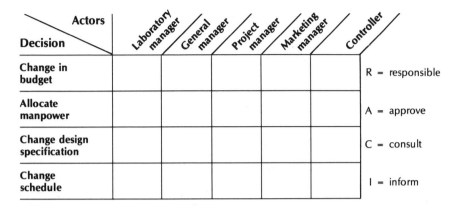

Actors / Decision	Laboratory manager	General manager	Project manager	Marketing manager	Controller	
Change in budget						R = responsible
Allocate manpower						A = approve
Change design specification						C = consult
Change schedule						I = inform

Figure 2. Example of a responsibility chart.
(Jay R. Galbraith, *Organization Design*, © 1977 Addison-Wesley Publishing Company, Inc., Reading, Massachusetts. Figure 2. Reprinted with permission.)

bly, this triggers some explicit attention to the meaning of individual versus group decisions, when each is appropriate, the practical limits of formal power, the risks and payoffs of acting without consulting others, and whether consensus means "doing what the group wants."

I find consensus decision making the least understood and most useful dimension of teamwork. Consensus means support is derived from each person's feeling heard and understood. A unanimous decision is a desirable goal; with or without unanimity, a boss has the responsibility to decide. This task is made easier if each team member feels free to speak openly about important matters. Indeed, the simplest team building technique is the "go around," in which each person is given the chance to say how he or she views a situation and what that person recommends doing. Bosses can facilitate this task by openly sharing their own dilemmas and willingness to hear what persons have to say. To maintain team cohesiveness, each person should be satisfied that he or she had a chance to influence the decision and declare a willingness to support it. When any team cannot do this, the team has a serious problem.

The future of team building

A team building meeting can be run simply and directly, or it can become a procedural nightmare of consultant-orchestrated exercises. My partner Tony Petrella, for example, has over the years reduced such meetings to essentials, seeking to make responsibility firmly rest with the team members. In one variation, the consultant simply interviews each member in front of the others, asking questions all have decided upon in advance. Everybody takes notes. People review their notes alone or in subgroups and diagnose their team's needs and priorities, with the consultant sometimes joining them. The diagnoses are discussed, agenda are built, and the remaining time is spent solving problems, working out new relationships, and/or improving policies and procedures. In another variation, Petrella and a colleague interviewed managers and wrote down everything they heard—a traditional approach—and in a follow-up meeting, rather than unveil their notes, they simply asked those attending to repeat for one another what they had told the consultants. This request was carried out enthusiastically.

The objective of these simpler procedures is to reduce passivity and put people more firmly in charge of their own lives. The consultant's role is to help persons talk constructively about their work, and to learn something new while doing it. I share Petrella's conviction that most people can devise their own solutions to organizational problems as readily with just a little outside help as with a lot. If you consider the "right" answer to be the best one that can be implemented, then I recommend this "less is more" approach for any situation in which participation and commitment are important to success.

Team building meetings are appropriate for any form of improvement activity. Teamwork is essential to the success of large systems. One would be mistaken, however, to assume that entire large systems change strategies can be built exclusively from this method. Team building is an important activity, but it is not enough. It makes most team members feel a greater sense of belonging, more influential, more competent, more supported, and more committed to their common enterprise. Following team building they may come away having solved some problems or obtained a new strategy, vision, or structure. They are still stuck, however, with the dilemma of implementing action involving those not present at the meetings. How well this is resolved depends on how well the team members have gotten together themselves.

REFERENCES

Galbraith, J. R. (1977). *Organizational design*. Reading, MA: Addison-Wesley.

Harrison, R. (1971). Role negotiations. In W. Burke & H. Hornstein (Eds.), *The social technology of organization development*. Washington, DC: NTL Institute/Learning Resources.

The Team Performance Model

Allan B. Drexler
David Sibbet
Russell H. Forrester

What do the U.S. Supreme Court, the starting five of the Indiana University basketball team, a crack business project group, and the Twelve Apostles have in common? Each

- is a team,
- shares common goals,
- has members from various backgrounds,
- faces an ambiguous situation in which values may conflict,
- must choose from among various ways to achieve the same goals,
- must perform a complex task requiring a high degree of interdependence and cooperation among the group members, and
- needs the highest level of performance for the team to achieve its stated goals.

If your work or consulting team shares these qualities, the team performance model outlined in this chapter will provide a useful tool for thinking about and diagnosing your team's performance.

Many successful teams are not like the Twelve Apostles or the Supreme Court. Syzmanski's Anne Arundel County champion duckpin bowling team is wonderfully accomplished, but is a high-performing team in a different sense: Its overall performance is simply the aggregate of the individual efforts of each of its bowlers, with almost no interplay occurring among them, except for moral support. Assembly line workers in a sewing machine manufacturing plant may be more interdependent than Syzmanski's bowlers, but their relationships are relatively simple and straightforward: Each worker contributes to the product as it passes down the line. The bowlers and assembly line workers face little ambiguity about the task or how to do it. These groups may succeed fully without becoming high-performing teams in the sense in which we use the term.

Changes in our world are bringing changes to teams. Society is more heterogeneous, and aging. More organizations are international, multidisciplinary, diversified, and regulated. And the work being done is centered more on information management and service rather than production. Teams are becoming more like the starting five of Indiana University's basketball team and less like Syzmanski's bowling team. That is, they are highly interdependent, engage in complex relationships, and work toward common goals with imperfectly matched values and different ideas about how they ought to do things. The Team Performance Model offers the most to teams with these characteristics. The model provides a way to map the significant things happening in a team, identify symptoms of destructive or counterproductive activity, and prescribe actions to move the team toward high performance.

The Team Performance Model

The Team Performance Model integrates Jack R. Gibb's original research on group behavior (Bradford, Gibb, & Benne, 1964) with the process theories of Arthur Young (1976a, b), a cosmologist who devised a comprehensive system for understanding the relationship between physical law and the human experience.

Working in the 1940s and 1950s as one of the pioneers of applied behavioral science, Gibb studied a large number of groups and discovered that people bring the following four basic concerns to all social interactions:

- the acceptance concern, which is related to the formation of trust, the acceptance of oneself and others, a decrease in anxiety, and an increase in confidence (this concern in part involves membership and degrees of membership in an organization);
- data concerns about the flow of perceptions, feelings, and ideas through the group and the individual, and the social system for expressing them;
- the concern for goal formation—the process of group goal setting, problems solving, and decision making—and the integration of the intrinsic motivations of individuals (goal setting in part involves productivity, having fun, creating, learning, and growing); and
- the control concern for the mechanisms by which activities are regulated, coordinated, and put into a useful sequence.

In Gibb's scheme, these modal concerns remain throughout the life of a group. They cannot be disposed of for good. The modal concerns are highly interdependent; success in dealing with one set of issues clearly affects the ability to deal with others. For example, when an organization has not resolved basic membership issues, it can hardly have the kind of free flow of data that supports good decision making. In theory, the four primary categories of concerns are neat abstractions; in real life, they are messy and do not come compartmentalized, arranged in a fixed hierarchy or sequence. However we find them, they remain the fundamental themes that all teams must continually address. How they are resolved always affects how well a group works.

Working in a different venue, Young set out in the early 1930s to develop a unified theory of how universal systems relate to one another. A physicist, mathematician, and inventor (he invented the Bell Helicopter, the world's first commercially licensed helicopter), Young was caught up in the general efforts of the early 20th century to describe a unified field theory integrating the major findings of science. After much research, he came to see that the unity of things is not found by examining the level of forms and structures, but by appreciating the nature of process. That is, all processes—small or large, internal or external—represent a constant dance between freedom and constraint, order and disorder, entropy and negentropy. This fundamental relationship between uncertainty and certainty lies at the heart of today's quantum physics, and is the underlying framework of process theory.

The Team Performance Model integrates the seminal work of Gibb and Young. Gibb discovered that the establishment of trust and acceptance, agreement about goals, procedures, and timing, and the exchange of information are all necessary elements of the group. That discovery fits with Young's observation that each process begins with some unexpressed potential, which begins moving in some direction, eventually joining other forces, until it can center on an identity, thereby creating the conditions for forms to combine into more complex arrangements.

Gibb articulated the fundamental concerns (acceptance, data, goal formation, and control) that influence the formative processes of all groups. Young's complementary notions that all process is movement from freedom to constraint and that evolutionary process is regaining freedom by mastering constraint give us a basis for describing a mature team's further growth. For example, what happens when a team begins to "click," breaking through the boundaries of individual limitation to reach a higher level of performance—sometimes referred to as synergy—and how does a team that has achieved real success renew and sustain itself?

The following is the basic pattern described by the model. A team's formative processes of initial involvement and identity formation tend to constitute movement toward increasing constraint. As a team defines its work and makes choices, boundaries are created. But when a team decides on its direction and moves to implement and maintain activity, it seems to journey back toward freedom. This is particularly true for teams that successfully resolve the concerns of the relevant stages. In sports, business, and government, high performance is associated with breaking the boundaries of individual capacity and somehow transcending the limits of our plans and language. Helping teams think about this whole range of possibilities is one aim of the Team Performance Model.

Graphically, the Team Performance Model looks like Figure 1. The model has seven primary elements, each representing a set of concerns team members face as they work together. For each element, the model describes some symptomatic behaviors that signal whether or not the concerns of that element have been resolved.

The elements of the model are interdependent; the progression from Stage 1 to Stage 7 is not chronological. All of the concerns represented in the model are constantly in play, although their salience at any time varies for each team. The general progression through the stages is one of dependence: Resolution of the issues of earlier stages enables the concerns of later stages to come into focus and be handled successfully. This dependence is not absolute, for any given team may succeed without resolving the concerns of one or more stages. In general, however, success at one stage makes success at another stage more likely.

The level of resolution for any of the concerns described by the model varies for most teams in two respects. First, differences usually occur among individual team members in how they resolve their concerns. On many teams, however, the members share an idea of how the team is doing with a given set of concerns—that is, all can perceive a "center of gravity." Second, the level of resolution for any set of concerns varies over time for most teams, and issues that have been settled can be reopened by design or circumstance. A breakdown in one area can have unsettling effects in another.

The model simplifies this complex reality. To ease discussion, we discuss each stage separately.

Stage 1: Orientation

The orientation stage issues are membership and acceptance, which are fundamentally rooted in a person's own sense of self. The capsule question framed in the model for this stage, "Why am I here?" is the core question the individual must answer to begin the process of finding a place in the group.

One subset of issues addresses the individual's right to be in the group, and is linked with the question "Do I belong?" Few of us pass

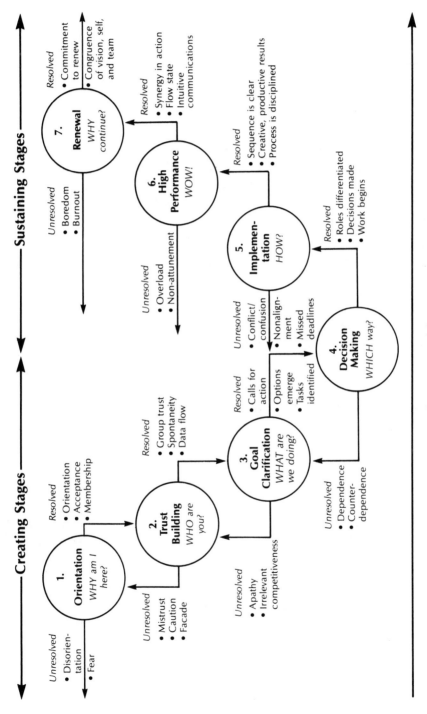

Figure 1. Team Performance Model™ (© 1987 Drexler/Sibbet)

through college without sometimes appearing in the wrong classroom at the wrong time and thus literally being out of place. Whenever anyone moves up—to a more responsible job, a better neighborhood, an advanced bridge level, or the like—the question "Do I belong in this league?" arises. Finding one's niche in a group requires the belief that one can make a contribution and offer something worthwhile as the basis of being accepted by the group.

The other side of the membership issue can be summed up in the question "Do I want to be here?" The core issue is whether the group is doing something one wishes to be a part of and which has some meaning for that person. To answer this question affirmatively, one must personally believe that the group's task is important and useful for the organization or for society—that is, that the product of the group's work has some utility. One also must believe that the team can do the task at least as well as—and preferably better than—the individual alone, or else the team has no real purpose. Finally, to resolve this issue positively, the individual members must be convinced that their skills will be used, their unique points of view will be heard, their membership will make a difference, and they will be able to influence the team's direction and outcome.

Sharing the conviction that its work will receive attention and be used can have dramatic effects for a team. We recently consulted with a police department on the East Coast as it set up a series of task forces to identify problems and recommend solutions to the police chief and commissioner. To each recommendation, the chief and commissioner responded in one of four ways:

- they accepted it and planned its implementation,
- they rejected it and explained why,
- they requested more time to consider it and responded later, or
- they asked for more information and provided a way to get it.

Not only were the task force members given complete and immediate feedback, but a full written account of their recommendations and actions was distributed to the whole police force. With this acknowledgment, the task force members were extremely motivated and could easily answer the question "Why are we here?" In fact, the task forces became high-performing teams. An interesting side effect of this response by the police chief and commissioner, discovered in later interviews with police officers, was the perception that more than two-thirds of the recommendations had been adopted whereas actually only 20% had been.

Each individual comes to a group with provisional membership, looking for a place and testing whether he or she fits with the group's purpose and other members. Resolving orientation issues is fundamentally important. Churches, civic institutions, fraternities, and sororities hold rites of membership. Athletes strive for a solid grounding before performing by "imaging"—that is, by literally seeing themselves in action. When members of work teams see themselves as fitting in and contributing to a worthwhile purpose, a different dimension is added to their work and part of the groundwork is laid for high performance. The members feel a sense of belonging or **membership.**

When a team's members cannot imagine a role for themselves, they tend to experience anxiety and fear. Nominal members who are misfits lacking any purposeful way to relate to others are disconnected from the group. They tend to focus on this lack of connection, making others feel uncomfortable. The internal conflict experienced by these marginal persons expresses itself in various dysfunctional ways. They may become withdrawn or distant from the group, or offer unsolicited criticism, never finding much value in the team's work. A typical example is that of a marketing specialist assigned to a manufacturing team to fill the vaguely defined role of a liaison-observer. This specialist experienced much distress trying to clarify her role in her own mind and adopting the passive role of a nonparticipant lacking full membership in the group. The custom of the military service academies of exchanging students so that they may serve as resident observers creates an even more challenging role definition problem. The visiting student lives within the other academy but continues to wear a home academy uniform. These exchange students invariably have difficulty conceiving of a comfortable role for themselves in the "foreign" setting.

When the members of a team feel they fit in and belong, they embrace the team's task and affirm their own participation in completing it. They find the basis for establishing relationships and defining their positions in the group. Resolving the orientation issues of Stage 1 frees them to address other interpersonal and task concerns.

Stage 2: Trust building

A striking example of a deliberate effort to build trust is that of a project manager of a newly formed team who began the team's first meeting by exposing his own hidden agenda to the group. Using prepared newsprint, he revealed not only his authentic work goals and purposes, but also some personal ones, such as using the experience to help obtain a promotion, the opportunity to travel to attractive resorts for meetings, and the like. He encouraged the other group members to reveal their own agenda so that together they could work on fulfilling as many of their organizational and personal goals as possible. Periodically, the team would refer to notes from this meeting to check its progress.

Stage 2 of the Team Performance Model concerns building trust, and the central question is "Who are you?" The hidden concern is "What will you expect of me?" An individual who is approaching the task with other members in the group needs to find out what they are like. Can they be relied upon? Do they know their craft? Can they maintain confidentiality? Are they genuinely dedicated to the task? Do they have ulterior motives? Will they accept my image of role and membership? In time, the team members show whether or not they are competent or open. When a group can answer these questions positively, trust tends to grow and be nurtured—otherwise an air of suspicion or skepticism generally prevails.

The example of the marketing specialist filling an observer role in a manufacturing team illustrates how resolving the issue of trust can center on one individual. Not only did the specialist experience role conflict, but her presence raised an issue for the whole team that eventually precipitated a confrontation. The participating team members worried about what and how the observer would report to others, and whether she was a "spy" from her department. The group managed to resolve this issue enough to enable the marketing specialist to become a productive team member. She did, however, have to undergo a rite of passage before gaining acceptance.

When a team is more heterogeneous, issues of trust can be more complicated. Consider the case of a pharmaceutical company that frequently sets up project teams to develop new products. These teams are interdisciplinary, reflecting the members' diverse academic backgrounds. The members' long-term interests and loyalties remain with their departments rather than with the project teams, which tend to have life spans of only several years. Typically, several members of a team arrive with hidden agenda defined by their department heads. One team's toxicologist sought to minimize the amount of time devoted to a particular project. The physician, looking ahead to taking over the project when it reached its clinical phase, was concerned about preparing for that time. The chemist sought to make the project a showcase for his department. For many months, these hidden agenda greatly disrupted the team. They were never discussed but were always present and restricted the team's interactive freedom. Through painstaking work, the team managed to reveal these hidden agenda, much to the members' relief. They remained real agenda, but the members were able to acknowledge individuals' interests and deal with them more rationally and openly.

Without trust, the flow of information on the task, goals, process, and means is diminished. Communication among members becomes calculated and measured. Information is withheld or distorted; persons may actually lie to one another. Members tend to keep up appearances notwithstanding reality, with no one saying the emperor has no clothes.

When group members trust one another, their interactions tend to be spontaneous, with little censoring of comments and reactions. Much information flows freely, and the group norm is that any valid feedback is acceptable.

A group's level of trust is not necessarily stable, but varies among members and over time. On one high-level military team, for example, the common tenor of group communications was formal, diplomatic, and deferential to rank. Occasionally, however, the group would move to another room and the commanding officer, an admiral, would remove his coat and light a cigar, with the others doing the same. The admiral would then raise some issues, express doubts or indecision, and invite reactions. The other officers would offer candid, unvarnished views. After this period of open exchange, the admiral would put his coat back on, reassert his rank, and announce his decision. The group then returned to its customary politeness. This group was unusual in being able—on signal—to achieve much spontaneity, openness, and data flow. The way it operated when the stripes of rank were removed is typical of teams that have basically resolved their issues of trust.

Most teams cannot do well unless their decisions are based on reliable information. If a project team's members distrust one another, the amount of good information available to them will diminish—along with the quality of their work. Trust building is a team's foundation; it is crucial to all of the other task issues identified for the following stages.

Stage 3: Goal clarification

Sometimes teams have precise charters, such as replicating an established product line or conducting a specified market survey. More often, within a broad purpose, the team has much freedom to choose exactly what it must do. (Frequently the team will benefit from explicitly identifying those areas of freedom so that it can better sense its level of discretion and control of its job.) The central task of Stage 3 is to clarify precisely **what** the team must do. Agreement on its tasks cannot occur without the members' exchanging information. Even an apparently simple objective may mask many possibilities and variations. Fundamental Stage 3 concerns are surfacing all of the options, identifying all of the issues, and marshalling the reasons for choosing among them.

Peter Vaill has referred to a symphony orchestra, which most people would assume has a single, obvious goal: a high-quality rendering of a piece of music. In a particular instance, however, the conductor, who had become committed a year earlier to doing the piece, did not even want to be involved; the violin section viewed the concert as an opportunity to showcase itself; and, similarly, the woodwinds section believed the piece would provide a good showcase for itself. The result was a mediocre performance caused by a failure to identify the true goals of the members.

Another example more relevant to the kind of team we tend to work with is that of a project team assigned to install a new product line in a manufacturing plant. The goal was clearly stated, but some members assumed that the line would last about 15 years, until the time they anticipated the plant would close. The positions they took radically differed from those of others who intended to develop a line for the ages. These two factions remained at odds over what should be done because they never agreed on the team's specific goals.

Managers commonly make the mistake of assuming that everyone agrees on the group's goals and is operating from the same premises. On a general level, people often do agree. In any given case, however, many differences of opinion exist over what exactly should be done. A team can usually benefit from clarifying its goals and finding some consensus about its purposes.

When a team has not addressed clearly what it should be doing, or has not resolved the issue, its interactions tend to be marked by either apathy or irrelevant competition. Watch a meeting of a group with unresolved Stage 3 issues, and you will notice a lot of arguments and bickering about things that do not matter that much. You will also notice that some members are tuned out, uninterested, and disengaged. These "fight-or-flight" symptoms tend to persist until the group reconnects with its real task issues and develops a consensus about its work. Teams that do not move beyond this stage rarely find or sustain the energy to perform at a high level. Their energies dissipate over many tangential or conflicting activities, or become invested in competition for dominance in setting the groups' direction.

Project teams frequently fail to recognize the acceptability of members' having both personal and organizational goals for the team. For example, a project manager may consider the team experience a stepping stone to a managerial position, and an electrical engineer may value it as an opportunity to gain marketing experience or pick up some administrative skills. These kinds of personal goals make up many of the hidden agenda that keep people from trusting one another. Teams may become freed by acknowledging members' personal goals immediately, thereby allowing people to devote their energies to achieving these goals rather than to hiding or rationalizing them.

When a group can define its agenda clearly and achieve some consensus on it, it has a common vision to guide the organization of its works. Its energies can thus be directed outward toward the task, setting the stage for both structure and creativity.

Stage 4: Decision making

When goals are clear and options identified, a team is eager to act. The question then becomes "Which way?" Making this decision is the most constraining work a team faces.

One of our clients, a team in the food industry, took the time to list each task it had to perform to complete its job, designating all the persons with a role or potential role in getting the job done (responsibility charting). Each team member then drew a grid designating the role of each person listed with respect to the task (e.g., doing the task, being informed about it, holding veto power). The team then superimposed the grids, revealing many conflicts and tasks for which no responsible agent had been designated. The team spent days talking about and sorting responsibilities, finally reaching consensus on the role of each member with respect to each task.

An interdisciplinary team in a matrix organization developed, appropriately enough, a matrix displaying for each team member the messages that person was receiving from various sources. The messages from the boss, project manager, self, and other members addressed what each person's role ought to be for the project. Sorting the conflicting messages for each person led to a process of role negotiation and clarification, and showed that some tasks were not being covered at all. The team succeeded, partially because it got onto a surer footing by resolving role conflicts, overlaps, gaps, and divergent expectations.

Another team took the time to develop a stakeholders' strategic plan, whereby it listed all of the stakeholders for its project, how it would deal with them, and who should handle each activity. At its biweekly meetings, the team brought its plan up to date, making it a "living" document to work by.

Each of these three teams, in different ways, dealt with the issues highlighted for Stage 4 in the team performance model. In this phase of its planning, the team primarily addresses the directions its work will take and the principal method for dividing responsibilities. Who will do what? What will meet the team members' concrete needs? When a team chooses its approach, it often feels a sudden move toward freedom: Decisions begin to flow, work begins to progress. If a team does not test its overall approach through some system of rigorous planning and reality checking at this point, the overlooked conflicts and gaps will later be revealed and affect the team's ability to achieve its goals. It is here that the team **makes the turn** toward high performance and greater freedom.

Dependence and counterdependence are symptoms of the failure to decide collectively on a basic approach and to differentiate individual roles. One typically expresses dependence by disowning individual responsibility for the success of the team's job and acceding to others' preferences—particularly the team leader's—without approving or disapproving of them. As a result, the work and responsibility tend to shift to one or a few group members. Counterdependence also springs from a passive, uninvolved state of the individual, but it is expressed in hostile, antagonistic ways, such as attacks on any or every proposed course of action—without offering a feasible alternative—complaining, and sarcasm. Both dependent and counterdependent behavior signal a lack of internalized understanding of how work should proceed, priorities, and team members' roles.

The refining process of Stage 4 crystallizes the level of interdependence needed to reach the team's goal. Many groups require a high level of interdependence among individual members for the team to succeed. This is particularly true for interdisciplinary projects (such as the Manhattan Project), activities for which timing among several persons is crucial (such as a barbershop quartet), or tasks that are essentially cooperative (such as a football team seeking to complete a forward pass). When the task demands a high degree of interdependence, the issues of Stage 4 are important.

Some tasks—such as simple problem solving—do not require much interdependence. In these cases, a team should not strive for it, as interdependence has no moral value in itself. Insisting on a great deal of interaction and the appearance of interdependence when it is not needed is as much of a mistake as is foregoing the integration of a team's functions when they are highly interdependent. We recently consulted the head of a small department whose staff was resisting requests for frequent meetings and exchanges of information. Our study showed that the employees' work was largely independent, and that the insistence of unnecessary meetings was dysfunctional. The department head eventually changed her image of a properly functioning team and let herself be guided by the nature of the work.

Stage 5: Implementation

The question "Who's on first?" may have brought fame and fortune to Abbott and Costello, but it has brought down many managers of brightly conceived and potentially profitable projects. A typical example is that of the electronics division of a national corporation. This division had a bright idea: installing kiosks in shopping malls that would enable shoppers to make catalogue purchases using their credit cards. It also had the technology, and its engineers designed a state-of-the-art system. This product was marketed well, creating a demand that outstripped the company's production ability. But the firm did not know how to assemble a project team that would work and produce results within deadlines. That was its downfall.

For Stage 5 the primary issue is reflected in the question "How will things be done?" Who does what, and when and where? The key concern is the sequence of work. When addressing Stage 5 issues, a team is imposing order on its work and committing itself to a schedule. In doing so, it defines the work it must do—and simultaneously frees itself from ambiguity and relieves itself of the burden of choosing from among alternative tasks. When the sequence is understood, energy and attention can be devoted to the work itself.

The challenge of Stage 5 is to integrate a collection of related tasks into a smooth operation. The sequence and timing must be right; the parts must mesh well; the system must be in balance. Like a symphony orchestra, it is not sufficient for each part to be perfected all by itself: It must blend in with and match the whole, or else the symphony is spoiled. Several well-established tools exist for managing complex projects, including PERT charts, Gantt charts, and the critical path method. One may obtain inexpensive and expensive software packages for each of these techniques and for others. Whatever the technique used, the key to success is taking the time to impose some common process or means of discipline. Put simply, the team must set a clear schedule and stick to it.

When Stage 5 issues are resolved, team members know the sequence of activities and share well-disciplined processes. The team's operations are smooth and orderly. When a team does not organize its activities the results are predictable: Work is haphazard, some tasks are not done at all, and others are delayed. Confusion prevails, conflict abounds, deadlines come and go. The team leader is likely exhausted, the members are frustrated, and creative energy is spent wastefully.

We caution readers about doing Stage 5 tasks well: Teams face some risk when they assign tasks and schedule their completion so rigidly that the work becomes too segmented, making members see less reason to meet, share progress reports, and keep others informed. This distancing may come at a time when integration is vital. The team leader must ensure that the work remains integrated and that members keep sight of the project as a whole as it evolves. The most productive teams are those in which everyone has a clear picture of the overall process and knows how her or his part fits into the sequence.

Stage 6: High performance

Stage 6 differs from the preceding stages in that no clear issue is associated with it—because no one solution will enable a team to reach a state of true synergy. You can feel it when it happens, you can observe its effects—but it is not totally predictable. High performance is not a child of logic, and is commonly described as "one plus one equals three (or more)." Boundaries and individual limits are broken—actually transcended—things fall together, everything clicks, and people feel "We've got it!"

High performance seems to happen in one of two ways. In one way it is precipitated by a crisis and a team rises to the occasion. An example of this is an emergency room team in a large metropolitan hospital. The team consisted of doctors of various specialties, nurses, technicians, laboratory staff, and others. This team was not usually a cohesive team. When a situation demanded it, however, the members pulled together and functioned as a high-performing team to save lives. Usually, this performance level was sustained only for a short period—the length of an emergency—and unfortunately did not carry over into the team's daily interactions.

The team performance model deals not with high performance precipitated by a crisis, but with the outgrowth of work done by a team as it deals with mastering the earlier stages and being open to the effects of team chemistry, timing, and luck. This kind of high performance is relatively enduring, though not constant. A team can systematically work toward it, and to some degree expect and rely on it. In this sense, high performance is exemplified by the trained intuition of a crack management team, or the smooth work of a skilled sailing crew when they are "in the groove" and getting the most out of the wind. Each member—from the captain to the winch grinder—contributes, is necessary, and can feel that the work is perfect. This is the condition the crew strives for, and what many teams need to find: the "click" that means everything is just right.

High performance according to this definition is relatively rare. When a team achieves it, it exhibits a few features we can describe. One is the experience of being in a flow state, as in the sailing metaphor. One feels that everything is moving smoothly in the same direction, without any drag, hindrances, or encumbrances, that activity is focused and coordinated, and that the system is balanced. Intuitive communication exists, as experienced by many couples in long-term, good relationships—the "I-knew-you-were-going-to-say-that" phenomenon of speaking without words, anticipating the thoughts and needs of the other person. The ability to communicate intuitively evidently is a product of both openness and of paying attention over a considerable period of time, of some degree of affinity, of consistency in behavior. A third feature of high performance is synergy in action. The individuals in the group outdo themselves, feeding one another's creativity, building on one another, and accomplishing more than the aggregate of their individual talents alone would permit. High-performing teams either do **more** than they could accomplish individually (1 + 1 = 3) or do it **differently**, with a quality, depth, or dimension not otherwise possible. High performance goes beyond what a team might ordinarily do.

As odd as this might sound, high performance is not for everyone. When a project requires a great deal of interdependence among team members, and demands creativity and surpassing the boundaries of a discipline, high performance is a valid, maybe necessary goal. When the group's work is routine, maintenance activity that does not demand creativity, striving for high performance may be a mistake. If patterns are well established and acceptable, working for high performance may simply be a waste of time.

Stage 7: Renewal

At the end of a one-and-one-half year project installing a new product line, a team held a final three-day retreat. The agenda included a graphic reconstruction of the history of the team's work, exchanging mementos of the experience, and looking at the career paths and prospects of each individual. The members' spouses were also at the retreat, whose purpose was to celebrate the completion of the project and to begin each member's transition to the next phase of work life. This provided an opportunity and concrete way for the team members to ask, "Why continue?" They had the chance to look at whether their jobs and careers fit their lives and plans.

In a sense, to ask "Why continue?" is to revisit Stage 1, to reassess if the work is still worthwhile, still needs to be done, still has some personal value and meaning. One may ask this about a particular project, a job, an organization, or a career field. It deals more with the context of the work and its relation to one's life than with the work itself. If one answers the question positively, then the process of asking it is usually energizing. This puts the team back in touch with the meaning the work has for it and renews its commitment to it. If the answer is negative—we should not continue—then the process is freeing, enabling members to move on to something they consider worthwhile and releasing them from the vaguely uncomfortable commitment to an enterprise they do not want to be part of.

One client of ours, a partner in a venture to market seminars and workshops, sparked a revitalization in his company by demanding that his associates examine what the enterprise meant to them and how much they wanted to continue to invest in it. In another case, a small architectural firm in New York that traditionally was a high-performing organization had been troubled in recent years by dissension among the partners. Reassessing his career and what he wanted to get out of life resulted in one of the partners' selling his share of the business. This change enabled the firm to get back on track to high performance, and the architect to seek a situation that better matched his general goals and needs.

Whatever the outcome, a team will benefit from addressing the issue explicitly from time to time. The basic concern is whether congruence exists between what the individual is doing, what the team is doing, and what the individual considers meaningful or important for her or his life. Is doing this valuable in my life? Is this how I want to spend my time? Is it worthwhile? If the team finds a match between what it is doing and what it wants to do, its work will assume a different character; the team will find more enthusiasm and harmony within itself. If a team cannot answer these questions positively, its members will act like people dragged into doing what they do not like, who would prefer to be somewhere else. Boredom and burnout are the primary symptoms of a mismatch between the team's work and what its members really want to do. When they occur, the team must find some value in its work if it is to go on, or else draw its work to a conclusion.

Application and validation of the model

A model has little purpose unless it fits and is useful in the real world. Our primary use of the Team Performance Model was to guide our thinking and sort team behaviors as we conducted consulting and team building. Our initial experiences in using the model in consulting and the feedback we received from teams using it were uniformly positive. The apparent validity of the model suggested two courses of action: (1) to make an effort to validate the model in a more rigorous fashion, and (2) to seek a mechanism to enable work teams to monitor their own performance independently. The team performance inventory was developed to serve both purposes.

The team performance inventory is a diagnostic instrument based on the team performance model. By using it, a team can gauge its own level of effectiveness along each of the seven dimensions identified in the model. The team performance inventory is a 70-item questionnaire using an agree-disagree format, with seven 10-item scales. For each scale, the items represent a range of potential behaviors or attitudes, varied in intensity and polarity. Some typical items are, for example, "Most members of our team lay their cards on the table" and "Our team takes the time to understand problems before responding to them."

The inventory contains a secondary five-team scale that addresses the performance of the team leader, such as "Our team leader doesn't provide enough direction over what goes on in the group." Although the five leadership items are each components of one of the seven primary scales, they are also interpreted together to provide feedback on the team leader's contribution to a group's performance level. The inventory also assesses the level of interdependence the team requires to operate successfully. This measure enables us to interpret the data on the rest of the items in terms of the "ideal" level of interaction, and provides the team with an opportunity to address the issue.

The data collected so far provide preliminary support for the Team Performance Model. Comparisons of teams' Team Performance Inventory responses with independently collected interview data typically show a substantial correlation between the two. As data accumulate, they will be the basis for determining if the scales defined by the model match the response patterns of real work teams.

REFERENCES

Bradford, L., Gibb, J., & Benne, K. (1964). *T Group theory and laboratory method*. New York: John Wiley & Sons.

Young, A. (1976a). *The geometry of meaning*. New York: Delacourte Press.

Young, A. (1976b). *The reflexive universe*. New York: Delacourte Press.

Teams and the Management of Emotion

Gene Bocialetti

At a meeting of a team involved in designing a new production process, an engineer and a line worker engage in a series of obviously frustrating exchanges with each other. They speak increasingly louder and exhibit flashes of anger while the others sit by mutely. After an awkward silence, someone mumbles, "Let's try to be objective and rational here." Everyone feels embarrassed.

At an executive team meeting, the boss aggressively—and seemingly angrily—makes a point in response to a question. Even though he asked for questions, the others become silent and avert their eyes.

A department manager convenes those directly reporting to her so that they can discuss a budget problem. She is upset about some overspending and demands to know why it occurred. Little information is volunteered. Exasperated, the manager establishes several new, more stringent rules for approval procedures. Her subordinates all feel angry about the new procedures and the implied mistrust. The implementation of the rules is later passively sabotaged.

Those attending a problem-solving team meeting are cheerful and expressive. The chair presents the group with a complex problem. Teammates engage in the task creatively, building on one another's ideas, feeling free to bring up differing, even unpopular points of view. Everyone feels confident and positive about the solutions, which are quickly and successfully implemented.

The above scenarios illustrate that emotions[1] and emotional experiences are constantly present in organizational life. Moreover, the "coloration" these emotions lend to work can have—and often do have—dramatic effects on the quality of work life and on organizational effectiveness.

Although commonly accepted today, the maxim that "the whole person comes to work" has not been translated well into implications for managerial practice. Although many acknowledge that the "thinking and feeling person" comes to work, managerial and team leadership is still oriented more toward handling the "thinking" side of an individual or group than the "feeling" side.

Organizations are clearly "emotiogenic"—that is, one's presence and participation in them creates and promotes emotional experience. The literature variously refers to organizations as the "defense against persecutory and depressive anxiety" (Jaques, 1974); as "haunted house[s]" and an "interactive, symbolic, emotionally charged field" (Van Buskirk & Srivastva, 1984); as an "interpersonal underworld" in which feelings are not expressed directly but are transformed so that one finds their expression through the group's task behavior (Schutz, 1966); and as "garbage cans" likened to "organized anarchies where choices go seeking problems, issues and feelings look for decision situations in which they might be aired and decision makers look for work" (Cohen, March, & Olsen, 1972, p. 1).

Common sense tells us, too, that organizations provide a stage on which many important dramas of life are played. This is true both for day-to-day task accomplishment and in the context of a career. Careers have been and probably will continue to be, for many, the mainstays of identity and sources of self-esteem. In this ecology of the organization and the career, we observe aspirations, achievements, hopes, social connections, falling in love, anger, hate, winning and losing, the experience of closeness, excitement, sadness, fear, anxiety, and jealousy.

Though many, if not all, of these phenomena are inevitably present, they may not be obvious or even discernible. Nonetheless, they are important components of organizational life and can undermine work effectiveness. When properly managed, though, they can also be a force for quality of work life and productivity.

Taking this view, one can argue that because emotions are inevitably present **and** can affect productivity **and** the quality of work for better **or** for worse, emotions should be managed.

Nowhere are emotions more present, potent, and manageable than in the context of work teams. Work teams typically provide enough diversity—in member viewpoints and representation—and enough immediate contact through many face-to-face encounters to generate much emotion.

Work teams face a basic choice when they form to do work. They must choose whether to establish a group or team culture that expresses emotions or one that suppresses them (Kaplan, 1979). Irving Janis, in his book *Victims of Groupthink* (1972), reveals a fascinating side of group decision making in his discussion of foreign policy fiascoes. For example, Janis examined the decision of President John F. Kennedy and his advisors to invade the Bay of Pigs in Cuba in 1961. In examining how the group's operations produced the disastrous decision to invade, Janis cites suppression of personal doubts for fear of appearing "soft," avoidance of conflict, intimidation by Robert F. Kennedy, the president's charisma, and his advisors' need to be liked by the president. Clearly, in this case emotions affected the group of individually skilled and capable policy makers.

The norm in most organizations—and hence in the groups populating them—is to suppress emotions. One is occasionally permitted to express anger, exasperation, or frustration, but if this exceeds some vague limit either in frequency or severity, one can be viewed as someone "who can't handle it/oneself." Because most team members do not clearly know the boundaries for expressing such emotions acceptably, they try to be sensible and safe by expressing no emotions. As a result, we often receive subtle and powerful messages to conform to the norm of suppression, including "Let's be objective here" and the popular "I don't think there's any need for emotional outbursts."

Such responses are not surprising. During childhood, our "primary socialization" gives us the basic template for adult behavior: the rules for living in society. Men especially get the normative message that men do not cry, not even when they are boys. Although this message is not as strong for women and girls, rarely are people encouraged to express the full range of emotions. When dealing with children and one another, adults have an amazing repertoire of behaviors aimed toward suppressing emotions.

This suppression has three effects in adulthood. One is that we cease to require others to help us suppress our emotions. We become skilled at suppressing them all by ourselves, internalizing the norm, and—with only occasional exceptions—living by it.

A second effect, aimed at preventing lapses in suppressing emotions, is that we tend to teach ourselves not to be aware of our emotions. We distance ourselves from them. We do not cease to have emotions or experience them, but simply stop being aware of how they affect us. During sensitivity training, people often have difficulty even **identifying the names** of more than three or four emotions (see the appendix for a sample of emotions). An example of this effect is the case of a manager I know who experienced a significant betrayal of confidence by someone he trusted. When I asked him how he felt about it, he responded, "I have no feeling at all about that." Only after I pointed out his rigid posture, furrowed brow, clenched teeth, and shallow, rapid breathing did he get a glimpse of the rage and hurt he felt. His refusal to engage in any more expressive activity allowed those emotions to continue taking a large toll on his body.

A third effect is that we learn little about managing emotions, either our own or others'.

"Controlling" emotions

People often protest, "Look at what happens when emotions are let out. People yell, get angry and upset, and work is disrupted." They notice that expressing emotions seems to have many undesirable effects, including the following:

- intimidating and frightening others,
- embarrassment, becoming the focus of attention,
- overstating one's views,
- provoking defensive or hostile responses,
- reflecting self-absorption, overconcern with oneself,
- loss of control of oneself,
- distracting others from "real" work,
- disruption or termination of relationships.

Without a doubt such effects do occur, illustrating the potentially harmful consequences of expressing emotions, particularly highly charged ones. One can argue, however, that such explosions are made even more likely—if not inevitable—by the chronic, reflexive suppression of emotion. Low to moderate levels of avoiding expression encourages the stockpiling of emotional energy. This continues until it becomes intolerable, and then a high-voltage discharge—much like lightning—occurs. Accumulated emotions are truly disruptive and often destructive. They often become aired at inopportune times or become directed at undeserving persons or issues. One should bear in mind that avoiding positive sentiments is just as common. People fear the following may result from of expressing such emotions:

- looking silly and awkward,
- being uncomfortable and violating norms,
- appearing naive,
- feeling too close too quickly,
- becoming the butt of jokes (e.g., "Why don't you two kiss?"),
- appearing "unbusinesslike,"
- appearing seductive (a problem in both heterogeneous and homogeneous groups).

Because of this, promoting emotional "control" does not actually imply control at all, in the managerial sense. If such promotion actually encourages the suppression or removal or emotions, one promotes **one** outcome regardless of the situation. One does truly consider whether such "control," or suppression, is necessary, desirable, or useful. Thus, this reflexive response can actually be a form of acting **out of control**, of an involuntary reflex action.

Costs of suppression

Suppression has its costs as well. Suppressing negative affect can have the following undesirable outcomes:

- internal body and psychological stress,
- withdrawal from participation,
- loss of energy and depression (when anger is directed inward),
- reduction of learning (remember the Bay of Pigs situation),
- important data for work is hidden,
- problems (and emotions) fester, often affecting implementation,
- opportunities to influence others are lost (messages carrying clear, responsible, and appropriate emotional "loading" are memorable and more likely to be influential).

Suppressing positive emotions can have the following undesirable outcomes:

- keeping others from being affirmed and recognized,
- dampening motivation,
- weakening the basis for receiving critical or negative affect or feedback,
- causing one to lose influence, as people tend to be more open to influence in an environment that is explicitly affirming.

Thus far, I have argued that emotionality exists in teams whether we like this or not. Because it exists, it must be managed by neither chronically suppressing emotions nor allowing them to be vented in ways that totally disrupt the team's work. Skillful managers of emotions can help teams work more effectively—that is, to do higher-quality work more quickly and become more productive—and can create a better climate (quality of work life) for everyone.

How to manage affect

This section is written for those readers participating in organizations and/or teams. Consultants will find it a good outline for giving short talks on managing emotionality in teams.

To manage affect, one must consider the timing, context, and extent of releasing emotions. By "extent," I mean one can choose to refer to the emotion(s) present, and to release a little, some, or all of it depending on the needs of the situation.

Timing. Generally, a good rule to follow is that expressing emotions in some form should follow the experiences engendering the emotions—or one's awareness of the emotions—as soon as possible. This is because true availability for work, personal presence, and participation begin to diminish as soon as emotional distraction occurs. If a lull in a conversation occurs, or if the group gets stalled, this may provide an opportunity to make a statement about emotions. A good time for this is often at the end of a team meeting. Team members then have greater freedom to listen, as their work is generally winding down. They also have more time to absorb what they hear and perhaps to decide on changes in operation before their next meeting.

Good timing may be affected by an obvious, noticeable—by several or all team members—signal that someone is experiencing strong emotions or emotional impairment. If a team member suddenly and evidently goes "blank" or becomes visibly upset, this may mean that the moment has come for pausing and taking stock of what is happening. The affected person(s) may well have become disengaged, at least temporarily, and this can be contagious. Such emotional experiences often start chain reactions, depending on which group members are close to, or identify with, the obviously affected person. Group concentration on the task will suffer until this is handled in some way.

Context. The best context in which to express oneself is the team itself. Sometimes, however, a team may not be ready for such expression. In such cases, some legitimizing activity may be useful. For example, at an appropriate time one may say, "I know we haven't talked about this in the group, but when the idea of [x] came up, I got pretty upset," "When I was reprimanded, I felt embarrassed," or the like.

Another context is a postmeeting talk with the team member who said or did whatever it was that engendered one's feeling(s). One should be careful to inform other team members of this if the emotional exchange was either noticed by others—this aids in legitimizing such expression—or if it affects the group's ongoing work.

Two other alternatives, presented in order of their effectiveness and desirability, are the following.

- Mention the event and your reaction to it to someone you trust who was there. This can provide a "reality check" and give you a source of support.

- Mention the event and your reaction to it to someone you trust who was **not** there, also to get a reality check and a source of support. Be careful, though: Because your confidant was not present and must rely on the data you supply, this person can only offer limited assistance in checking reality. Also avoid starting "satellite communications"—that is, do not ask, encourage, or allow your confidant to carry your message to others. **You** must manage it. Messengers often distort meanings, and the presence of others begins to politicize relations and can polarize teams. Ultimately, this can cause factions to arise on a team.

Extent. Most people think in binary, either/or terms about emotional expression: Either one expresses one's feelings fully or not at all. One has, however, many more choices than this. I consider it useful to think of emotional expression in terms of a continuum.

Before discussing the continuum, I emphasize that making no expression at all—in any form—should remain an option for teams at work. I am not against this, but simply consider this choice overused. In certain kinds of situations, however—such as that of a short-lived group with a noncreative task whose relations will not endure once the work is completed—the best option may be to refrain from emotional expression.

On one end of the continuum, one may express feelings in abstract terms without using other cues. In doing this, one refers to a feeling by using words, leaving out appropriate facial, tonal, and body cues. A simple declarative statement such as "I am angry with you" is used.

Although this action identifies one's feeling and lets others become aware of it, it has a few disadvantages. Because of the lack of other cues, it is sometimes unconvincing. People are not greatly inclined to be affected by it, and perhaps will not take it seriously. It may also confuse others because the words may seem to say one thing while the face, tone, and body fail to reinforce this, indicating instead the absence of feelings.

In the midrange on the continuum of expression, one may refer to one's emotional experience by using some nonverbal cues—thereby lending one's message force and credence—yet without expressing the full charge of one's emotions. The message remains primarily verbal, but contains appropriate, congruent cues. To the statement "I am angry with you" one would add tensed facial muscles, furrowed eyebrows, and direct eye contact with the recipient of the message. One may possibly move one's body forward toward the other person.

On the end of the continuum reflecting the fullest expression of emotions, the release of one's feelings occurs more spontaneously and is both verbal and nonverbal, with the volume level of one's voice raised. This form of expression is most satisfactory for relieving the sender's tension, and has the maximum impact for delivering messages and getting attention. It requires, however, a moderate to high level of skill by others in managing the exchanges following it. When such expression is made in a group that is not well developed and/or trained, it will likely provoke a defensive response by the recipient of the message and a feeling of helplessness by the rest of the team.

Choices in emotional expression

I wish to make one further point about the choices we can make and encourage in emotional expression: No one can "make" another person feel anything. We can, and ought to, choose whether to feel or not to feel, and what to feel. Similarly, we can choose to pay attention to or ignore our emotional experiences. Finally, as I say above, we can choose how and whether to express our emotions and to what extent.

Choosing to manage one's affect has several advantages. For one, **this creates internal comfort**. Psychic stress is kept at lower levels on the average, and one can deal with problems more easily if the attendant emotional charge has been kept at modest levels through periodic "expressive maintenance."

Second, **interpersonal and work relationships are more stable and closer**. Less emotional baggage clutters up one's interactions or interferes with one's work, resulting in more effective and pleasant relationships.

Third, **work groups improve their effectiveness** and are more consistently high performers. Problems of withdrawal, boredom, and frustration are much less likely to overwhelm the team.

Acquiring skills in expression is timely, as many organizations are changing their ways of operation to deemphasize status and authority and encourage more open expression of divergent viewpoints. An inevitable corollary of this change is that emotional presence and strength are likely to increase. Furthermore, organizational concerns about employee stress, "Type A" behavior, accident rates, and productivity all point toward a freer approach to dealing with emotionality, as bottled-up emotions can be destructive. Even when organizations continue to support emotional suppression, individuals can fashion their relations by using a different set of rules supporting expression.

Another reason to promote freer expression and management of emotions at work relates to their effects on the nonwork spheres of one's life. Two phenomena commonly occur. One is that emotions bottled up at work often explode at home, a displacement that is both unjust and impractical, as it leaves work problems unsolved and victimizes innocent parties. The second phenomenon is the suppression of a broad range of affect both at work and at home. I argue that suppression **often** has negative consequences in the work place, but **always** has negative consequences in the home and in personal relationships with one's spouse or lover, other family members, and friends.

Finally, one should remember that opening up the negative end of the range of emotions—which contains such feelings as fear, anger, and hurt—and learning to managing this competently leads to opening up the positive, relationship-building emotions such as admiration, appreciation, praise, excitement, laughter, and enthusiasm. These positive emotions create color in relationships and keep them from becoming either negative or "gray," listless, and unexciting.

In sum, our emotional expression is what makes us interesting, colorful, creative people. It makes work more exciting, meaningful, and fun, and makes life more worth living.

NOTE

1. In this chapter, the terms "emotion" and "affect" are used interchangeably.

REFERENCES

Cohen, M.D., March, J.T. & Olsen, J.P. (1972). A garbage can model of organizational choice. *Administrative Science Quarterly, 17,* 1-25.

Jaques, E. (1974). Social systems as a defense against persecutory and depressive anxiety. In G.S. Gibbard, J.J. Hartman, & R.D. Mann (Eds.), *Analysis of groups* (pp. 177-299). San Francisco: Jossey-Bass.

Janis, I.L. (1972). *Victims of groupthink.* Boston: Houghton-Mifflin.

Kaplan, R.E. (1979). The utility of maintaining work relationships openly: An experimental study. *The Journal of Applied Behavioral Science,* 15(1), 41-59.

Schutz, W.E. (1966). *The interpersonal underworld.* Palo Alto, CA: Science and Behavior Books.

Vanbuskirk, W.R., & Srivastva, S. (1984). *The organization as haunted house: Heat and emotional positioning in corporate cultures.* Unpublished manuscript, Western Carolina University, North Carolina.

BIBLIOGRAPHY

Denzin, N.K. (1984). *On understanding emotion.* San Francisco: Jossey-Bass.

Gustafson, J.P. (1977). Injury to the self-concept in the working small group, in perspective. *Journal of Personality and Social Systems,* 1(1), 39-52.

Zajonc, R.B. (1980). Feeling and thinking: Preferences need no inferences. *American Psychologist, 35*(2), 151-175.

APPENDIX

Sample of emotions

pleasure	sadness
satisfaction	pride
boredom	frustration
jubilation	remorse
fear	disgust
daring	depression

jealousy	happiness
excitement	repulsion
loneliness	love
elation	gratitude
silliness	incompetence
hesitation	guilt
surprise	elation
envy	hopelessness
eagerness	hate
weariness	spite
anger	adventurousness
gladness	inspiration
grief	joy
contentment	exasperation
confidence	amazement
anxiety	helplessness
solemnity	rejection
apathy	motivation
hope	feeling overwhelmed

Do You Have ROCS in Your Head? The Illusions of Rationality, Objectivity, Consciousness, and Separability in Team Building

Nancy L. Brown

In building effective teams, those involved—especially the leaders—must base their efforts on firm ground. This chapter addresses the firmness of that ground—that is, the correctness of the beliefs individuals and organizations hold about the nature of people, work, and teams.

In the Western world, some team-building assumptions serve us well, but others lead us to create teams and plans that do not work. The inaccurate assumptions, which I address in this chapter, I label illusions, or myths. The four most central myths blocking effective team development in North America and Europe are the illusions of rationality, objectivity, consciousness, and separability (ROCS).

The **illusion of rationality** is the belief—held by most managers and consultants—that the team's and organization's essential processes of perceiving, analyzing, and making decisions are rationally based, or related primarily to facts and deductive logic. This illusion contrasts with reality, in which large elements of emotion and intuition are present, although often unacknowledged.

The destructiveness of the illusion of rationality lies in its invitation to ignore emotion and intuition in the team's workings, and thus (1) to leave out two important tools needed by the team and (2) to lead the team to establish plans that are not well founded, that do not fully con-

---

sider the emotions and intuition of team members and key stakeholders.

Consider the following example of a marketing team developing a proposal for the next year's goals. The group fails to consider that one of the decision makers is angry because he was chewed out by his manager the week before about extraordinary media costs. By not considering this, the team fails to include in its proposal information about the efficiency of money to be spent on media costs. The angry decision maker vetoes the proposal.

Sound team building surfaces and uses relevant emotions and intuition, as well as facts and deductive logic.

The **illusion of objectivity** is the belief that an "objective reality" exists and can be seen and understood—if one is smart enough and removed enough from the situation. This illusion contrasts with the reality that a variety of perceptions are present, each inherently subjective. Individuals can see a situation more accurately when they clear away internal factors that distort or block information. But even when a group of persons does much of this self-clearing, they still hold varying perceptions of the situation.

The illusion of objectivity becomes destructive when it leads a team to spend inordinate amounts of time, energy, and other resources on seeking "the objective answer." Sometimes the team attempts to do this by bringing in an outsider to give the team an "objective" viewpoint. What the team and the outsider regard as more objective is merely distant from the team and less related to its history than the team members' viewpoints. The outsider's view may or may not be more accurate; it **is** yet another subjective perception.

Spending too much time, energy, and resources occurs when a team attempts to uncover and resolve its members' differing perceptions beyond the point of necessity. The team wastes time and reduces quality when it defers to someone in a position of authority over the team, as if—merely by rising in the organization—this person had cornered the market on "objective truth." The illusion of objectivity is destructive not only in wasting time and reducing quality, but also in diminishing the team's creativity and fun by devaluing differences among team members.

Sound team building reminds team members that seeking accurate information is useful only up to a point, and that no amount of information can, or should attempt to, dissolve differing perceptions into one "universal truth." A wise consultant treats her or his own perception as just one additional view—not necessarily one that is better than that of any team member.

The **illusion of consciousness** is the belief that the factors influencing perception and decision making—such as hopes, fears, and motives—are fully conscious and known by the actor(s) before and during the processes of perceiving and decision making. This illusion contrasts with the reality that all of us as individuals, teams, and organizations are moved by factors that are both conscious and unconscious.

The illusion of consciousness is destructive when it (1) leads persons to ascribe intent inaccurately, (2) leads to ill-founded strategies for change, and (3) limits the approaches considered for influencing others.

For example, a manager named Margaret wants to finish reviewing her subordinates' performances well before her deadline of June 30. Consciously, she is motivated by knowing that finishing early will leave her more time to handle her budget proposals, also due in June. She is not aware, however, that she is conducting the performance reviews first because that allows her to postpone until later the less exciting and less pleasant tasks of the budget.

A schedule for the budget work, performance reviews, and other key tasks is to be set at a team building session at the beginning of the year. Margaret's subordinates want her to conduct the reviews in June. If they take her conscious and spoken rationale to indicate Margaret's full motivation, they may suggest that she develop her budget proposals in May so that they will not crowd her work on the performance reviews in June. This strategy would not consider Margaret's unconscious dislike for budget work or her unconscious preference for postponing unpleasant tasks. Their strategy would not work well because it would assume that Margaret knows and can articulate all of what motivates her. I suggest that in many cases this is not possible.

Sound team building explores issues of intent, with the understanding that humans rarely grasp consciously all of their own motives. It takes into account the influence of unconscious motives and emotions of individuals **and** of teams.

The **illusion of separability** is the belief that one's performance can be separated from those of others on one's team, or that the performance of one's team can be separated from those of other teams. A corollary illusion is that one's contribution therefore can be measured separately, yet still accurately. This contrasts with the reality of blurred boundaries between one person's contribution and those of others. If your "output" becomes my "input," our contributions cannot be fully separated from each other, nor separately measured or rewarded accurately.

Of the four myths of rationality, objectivity, consciousness, and separability, separability is the most difficult to address. It is embedded in Western culture in the way we select, develop, and reward organization members. Although the term "synergy" is often used, our organizations actually seldom leave team membership intact long enough for teams to develop synergy, let alone use it. (Synergy occurs when, through cooperation and inspiration, the whole becomes greater than the sum of its parts, and the team produces more and better work than the sum of its individual members' work.)

The illusion of separability becomes destructive when it leads teams to spend excessive time pursuing "simple and equitable" ways of measuring and rewarding individual contributions. Team members thus become so focused on whether their own contributions are being judged accurately that they become insufficiently focused on the team's task. Also, team members may spend energy competing dysfunctionally, energy that could be devoted to work on the task.

This illusion is also destructive when it leads to "compartment thinking" rather than "systems thinking." Compartment thinking occurs when one draws false boundaries among organizational issues, seeing each issue contained fully in its own neat box. Systems thinking, however, occurs when one sees how one organizational issue is connected to—and influenced by—others. For example, systems thinking lets you see the effects of morale in your work group on the productivity of mine.

Sound team building acknowledges the impossibility of separating fully one's performance from those of others. This provides a backdrop against which appropriate levels of role clarity and accountability are sought.

In summary, when building a team, a leader—or consultant—must be alert to when one or more of the above myths may be operating and hindering the team. This requires that one also be alert to the presence of these illusions in one's own mind. Once you recognize that such a myth is operating in your own thinking, the task of helping the team will become easier. Frequently, you can intervene effectively by saying what you perceive, and then inviting others to explore the perception. Once the team discusses the presence or absence of such a myth in its own work, it can adjust its assumptions and move on to more productive work.

Team Building as Group Development

Philip G. Hanson
Bernard Lubin

I. Overview

Teams: Where do you find them? Although one may describe and approach work teams in various ways, we focus on their group characteristics and processes. This perspective enables us to use four decades of knowledge and skill to improve the productivity and work relationships of work teams.

Every organization consists of work teams, or—at least—a single work team. Teams consist of persons who have some relationship with one another or reason for working together as a function of doing their jobs or accomplishing a task. Some teams are relatively permanent, such as that of a supervisor and subordinates, a manager and that person's supervisors, or a president and the vice presidents or top-level managers. Other teams are temporary, lasting only as long as necessary to accomplish a particular task; examples include task forces, committees, and the like. A person may belong to more than one team, as when a manager is part of both a management team and a team including the manager's subordinates. A team may also be dispersed throughout a large geographical area, particularly if it is part of a large organization with offices and plants in different locations.

Characteristics of a well-functioning team. Developing a well-functioning team takes considerable time and effort. Team members must recognize and accept their own needs and be sensitive to those of other team members, and maintain some balance among these needs. A principle of effective team functioning is that members must be highly concerned with both their own needs and others'. These needs are analogous to the major concerns of management for task and people (morale). The following are some of the characteristics of an effective team.

1. The team shares a sense of purpose or common goals, and each team member is willing to work toward achieving these goals.
2. The team is aware of and interested in its own processes and examining norms operating within the group.
3. The team identifies its own resources and uses them, depending on the team's needs at any given time. At these times the group willingly accepts the influence and leadership of the members whose resources are relevant to the immediate task.
4. Group members continually try to listen to and clarify what is being said and show interest in what others say and feel.
5. Differences of opinion are encouraged and freely expressed. The team does not demand narrow conformity or adherence to formats that inhibit freedom of movement and expression.
6. The team is willing to surface conflict and focus on it until it either is resolved or managed in a way that does not reduce the effectiveness of the individuals involved.
7. The team exerts energy toward problem solving rather than allowing it to be drained by interpersonal issues or competitive struggles.
8. Roles are balanced and shared to facilitate both the accomplishment of tasks and feelings of group cohesion and morale.
9. To encourage risk taking and creativity, mistakes are treated as sources of learning rather than reasons for punishment.
10. The team is responsive to the changing needs of its members and to the external environment to which it is related.
11. Team members are committed to periodically evaluating the team's performance.
12. The team is attractive to its members, who identify with it and consider it a source of both professional and personal growth.
13. Developing a climate of trust is recognized as the crucial element for facilitating all of the above elements.

Team building or team development. Calling a group or work unit a team implies that it has a particular process of working together, one in which members identify and fully use one another's resources and facilitate their mutual interdependence toward more effective problem solving and task accomplishment. Therefore, team building is an effort in which a team studies its own process of working together and acts to create a climate in which members' energies are directed toward problem solving and maximizing the use of all members' resources for this process. Perpetuating a climate in which individual resources are withheld and available energy drained by protective or defensive facades is counterproductive to effective team functioning.

To help a team study its own workings, managers sometimes hire OD consultants. If the managers have sufficient process skills, they may choose to help their teams themselves in studying how they function. Consultants or managers may use several approaches, including helping their teams develop a process orientation; using self-observation, data collection, and feedback; and assessing team members' leadership styles and their impacts on team functioning. One important aspect of team building is helping a team develop a "model of excellence" against which it can measure its own performance.[1] After identifying norms and procedures of team functioning, the team may then establish criteria for effectiveness along several behavioral and procedural dimensions, providing targets for team achievement. For team building to succeed, however, all team members must see the relevance of this self-study to more effective functioning, and be **committed** to perceiving and critiquing their own behavior.

Assessing the need for and conditions conducive to team development. Team building is indicated when managers and/or team members recognize certain symptoms. These symptoms include low productivity, unresolved conflicts among members that block team understanding and use up time, inappropriate use of member resources, unclear decisions, confusion as to who should do what and when, ineffective staff meetings characterized by little or no participation or problem identification, a general lack of interest and creativity, and complaints that the team does not respond to the needs of others—such as users or other departments—or meet its responsibilities.

When a team studies its own process and seeks to develop more effective ways of operating, it faces some risks. Such activity may cause conflicts and painful feelings that have been hidden for a long period to surface and produce tension and anxiety. Members may fear that their future relationships will be adversely affected by their "leveling" with one another and exchanging feedback. These risks, however, are more than compensated for by the benefits of getting issues "on the table" for examination, developing more authentic ways for team members to relate to one another, increasing team members' competence in handling interpersonal conflicts, and encouraging the team to use its energy for creative problem solving. For team development to be effective despite the risks, the following conditions must be met.

1. The leaders must be committed to and involved in team building. Team building cannot occur if a team has no formal leader or if its leader has an indifferent or cynical attitude toward the effort.

2. Team leaders must be willing to examine their own roles with respect to their teams.
3. All team members must be highly committed to the effort and willing to take responsibility for making it work.
4. All team members must be committed to studying the team's process and to critiquing their own performances. These two activities never end, but continue throughout the life of the team.
5. Team building is not possible without team (staff) meetings. When managers meet with subordinates individually and never hold regular team meetings, the team members cannot relate to one another as a group in direct, face-to-face interactions. When subordinates must communicate with one another through their managers, the managers can control the flow, direction, and content of the information.
6. Team building activities should not be limited to special sessions, retreats, or visits from a consultant, but should occur daily at work as team members demonstrate their commitment to putting into practice what they have learned.
7. Team members must understand that team building is not a one-time-only procedure, but rather a process of continuous diagnosis, action planning, implementation, and evaluation.

The team building consultation process. In general, team building involves several steps. If external consultants are hired, the team building process is initiated during the first contact between the consultants and the client managers as they determine what kind of assistance the clients need and how the consultants and clients will work together.

The consultants then may gather data on the team culture, learning how persons work together and the norms, values, beliefs, policies, and practices governing their behavior so that they can determine the current state of a team and the changes to be made to facilitate movement toward organizational objectives. To determine a team's current status, its traditions and norms must be made explicit. After collecting the data, the consultants diagnose it in terms of the team members' goals for improving the team's functioning. Then concrete interventions are planned and implemented, consisting of action steps for keeping, modifying, or dropping old norms and/or initiating new norms the team agrees to adopt. The results of the interventions are evaluated to measure how much the team has achieved its goals. Finally, follow-up evaluations are made periodically to track the team's progress and provide ongoing diagnoses for further interventions.

The total process, or parts of it, may be repeated in a cyclical pattern, with objectives changing to meet the team's needs as it changes.

II. The consultant assists with team building

The first meeting of the consultant and the client. The team building process begins when the manager or team leader feels the need to improve the team's functioning. The leader and some of the team members may already recognize some of the symptoms of ineffective functioning mentioned above. They may not, however, be sure about how to correct the situation. If the team leader has a big investment in changing this situation and is willing to accept the conditions required for effective team development, a consultant may be hired—if the manager lacks the necessary skills for conducting her or his own team development program.

During the first contact between a consultant and manager, the team building intervention begins. The consultant's questions may give the manager a new perspective on the problem. Moreover, the mutual exploration may permit a better assessment of the manager's degree of motivation toward being involved in the team building effort. At this time both the consultant and the client must decide how they will work together, share their expectations for one another, and determine how realistic these expectations are with respect to each person's competence and the goals of the team building effort.

Data gathering. Once a contract has been made to proceed with the team building, information must be collected to determine the current status of the team's functioning. The data must be relevant to the issues and problems perceived by the manager and team members (for example, individuals' personal problems at home are generally not relevant). Individual confidentiality must be protected, so a decision must be made as to which information to share with the entire team and make available for feedback.

Consultants may gather information in several ways. One is by observing the team working in its natural setting. This enables consultants to learn about the patterns of interaction and influence within a team, how decisions are made, how stress is managed, and how the team solves problems. Another is through individual or group interviews. If individual interviews are held, the consultant and the individual must decide which information can be shared with the entire team. A third method of collecting information is the use of questionnaires and survey instruments. These make the data collection appear objective and highlight the issues the team members find unsatisfactory and would like to change. Finally, one may use all three methods, combining face-to-face contact with the more "distant" questionnaires and survey instruments.

When gathering data, the consultant may use a combination of open-ended questions and rating scales. A sample of appropriate open-ended questions is listed below.

- What do you consider the real problems in getting the job done?
- What problems do each of the members cause you in getting your job done? Identify and describe the nature of the problem.
- How does the boss's leadership style affect the team's work?
- When differences in the team arise, how are they handled?
- Is feedback given to members who get out of line or have problems?
- How is conflict handled in the team?
- Does a spirit of trust and caring exist within the group?
- To whom do you usually go when you have a problem? Do you feel free to use persons from your section as resources? From other sections? If not, why?

Rating scales (see sample below) provide data that can be summarized and provided to the team without much risk to individual members. Using them allows team members to compare their own perceptions with everyone else's. If the data indicate large discrepancies between the current situation and what the team would like it to be, these can indicate how the team should start as they appear on the original form.

Table 1
Form B: How I See My Work Unit or Team (Selected Examples)*

In this section, you will be considering how you view **your particular work unit or team** within the organization. In making these ratings, you will be considering some of the same or similar items you have rated before (Form A), as well as some new items. This time, however, you will be focusing on the organizational work unit in which you do all or most of your work.

In rating each item, first circle the number on the scale that most closely approximates the way you see your work unit or team functioning **now.** Then, rate the item again, this time circling the number that best describes how you **would like** to see your work unit or team functioning. Remember: This time you are to rate the item in terms of **your** view of your work unit or team.

Goal setting:

Now	1	2	3	4	5	6	7
Would like	1	2	3	4	5	6	7
	Team or work unit goals set for us from above						Goals set by the team, emerging through team interaction and agreement

Participation:

Now	1	2	3	4	5	6	7
Would like	1	2	3	4	5	6	7

Table 1 (cont'd.)

One or two
persons dominate,
others are silent
or respond minimally

All team members
actively participate
as the need arises

Feedback:

Now	1	2	3	4	5	6	7
Would like	1	2	3	4	5	6	7

Little or no
sharing about how
well members are
working together,
or how they affect
team or work unit
effectiveness

Members ask for and
give feedback freely
and share how they
stand with one
another and how well
they are contributing
to team or work unit
effectiveness.

Decision making locus:

Now	1	2	3	4	5	6	7
Would like	1	2	3	4	5	6	7

Influential few
push through
decisions;
decisions made by
unit manager or
supervisor

All members are
encouraged to
participate in
decisions; full
agreement of team
is sought

Distribution of leadership:

Now	1	2	3	4	5	6	7
Would like	1	2	3	4	5	6	7

Much dependence on
on one or two
members or leader
to get things done;
others "wait and
see" without much
involvement

Leadership
distributed and
shared among team
members; individuals
contribute when
their resources are
needed

Problem solving:

Now	1	2	3	4	5	6	7
Would like	1	2	3	4	5	6	7

Little or no
attempt to look at
team issues or
problems; no real
diagnosis of forces
affecting work unit
functioning

Team diagnoses
problems and team
issues, critiques
its own effectiveness
and all the forces
affecting team
functioning

Handling team conflicts:

Now	1	2	3	4	5	6	7
Would like	1	2	3	4	5	6	7

No tolerance for
expression of
negative feelings
or confrontation;
conflicts
suppressed or
"swept under the
rug"

Negative feelings
and tensions
surfaced and
confronted within
the team; conflict
seen as potential
source of creative
team effort

Using resources of team members:

Now	1	2	3	4	5	6	7
Would like	1	2	3	4	5	6	7

Talents, skills, and experience of team members not identified, sought, or given recognition	Talents, skills, and experience of team members are fully identified, recognized, and used whenever appropriate

*These are sample items from an instrument entitled "Diagnosing Organizational Effectiveness" by Philip G. Hanson, Ph.D. and Antaro Richard Burke, Ph.D., copyright 1977, TMS Corporation, 5451 Lymbar Drive, Houston, Texas 77096.

After the data collection is completed, the consultant and/or the manager and team organize and evaluate the data. The consultant must keep in mind which data can and cannot be shared with the team; **the confidentiality and protection of individual team members must be respected in this situation.** Ways of presenting sensitive data exist so that individual confidentiality is preserved while the information is made available to the group.

Some consultants organize the data themselves, presenting them to the team in the form of profiles, charts, and tables. This gives team members a visual representation of their situation and can provide a starting point for evaluation and planning. Other consultants share responsibility with the team for organizing and presenting the data. The latter method has the advantage of immediately involving team members and training them to handle this type of activity themselves. Deciding which method to use may depend on the situation and time constraints. For example, the first method may be appropriate if the team and its manager are widely dispersed and will only come together for a short period, during which they must decide whether or not to engage in a team building effort. In this meeting the consultant may spend most of the time presenting the data collected and allowing the team members to discuss their implications.

Planning and problem solving. Once a diagnosis has been made and the issues to be addressed outlined, the manager and team must determine which issues take priority and should be worked on first. After the agenda have been set, the manager should take a more prominent role in the effort by conducting the planning and problem-solving phase. The consultant now acts as a process observer and facilitator, seeing how the group addresses the issues and uses its resources. The consultant can help the group look at its own problem-solving process, the extent to which task and maintenance functions are being monitored, and whether effective decision-making procedures are being used. Thus, the consultant helps the team become sensitive to its own internal processes and generate interest in analyzing these processes. As before, instruments can facilitate the analysis of the group's performance. As the group's trust level increases, however, team members may more openly express their opinions and feelings, and even ask for additional meetings devoted solely to examining interpersonal and group issues. That is, the team may move toward a training group format for examining these issues and for allowing members to provide one another with feedback. In addition to working with teams, consultants may also work with managers individually to help them improve their ability to observe and process data about themselves, learn from the feedback they receive, and solve their own problems.

Implementation and evaluation. For plans to be effective, they must be implemented. The manager is responsible for seeing that plans are carried out and for making the team understand that it is committed to the plans developed by the team. The manager and team must list the goals for the team building effort (e.g., the model of excellence) and determine which dimensions—such as individual and team behavior, work performance, and productivity—will be monitored to measure change. These goals should be described in ways allowing for measurement toward or away from objectives. During this phase, the consultant should actively share expertise in establishing ways to evaluate the program. Individual or group reports, observations, and instruments can again be used to collect data. The group and its manager must also determine how frequently to assess the immediate and long-term effects of the intervention, and keep in mind that team building is not a one-time-only event, but an ongoing process. The cycle of diagnosis, intervention, feedback, and evaluation must be repeated continually. Unless the team is committed to this never-ending process of critiquing its own performance, effective team functioning will deteriorate and old, ineffective habits will emerge again.

Identifying team members' leadership styles. For a team to function at its best, it must identify its resources and use them whenever and wherever appropriate. These resources reside in the team members. Whether or not they are fully used depends on **how** each team member presents them or which leadership styles are prevalent in the group. Some members are skilled in "getting the job done"; others are more effective in producing a climate of high morale. Some leaders tend to dominate and create dependency in others; others tend to be excessively supportive at the expense of filling their own needs; others manage to balance concerns for both tasks and people. Paying too much attention to one aspect of team functioning—either task or maintenance—to the detriment of the other may cause low morale and, consequently, low productivity. Therefore, the team leaders and members can best serve the team's goals if they recognize their own leadership styles, how these shift under different conditions (e.g., pressure, crises, slow periods), and their impacts on team functioning.

The role of the consultant in team development. In most organizations, team leaders do not have the necessary process and group skills to manage their own team building efforts. Moreover, the role of the team leader—and the ways in which the leader's style affects the team—must be open for exploration and feedback from team members. Without external consultants, team members will not likely confront their own managers if those managers are conducting the sessions. Most managers thus seek consultation from outside sources.

Using external consultants has several advantages and some disadvantages. For one, because they do not belong to the organizations, they are freer to respond to or comment upon team behaviors. Second, because consultants lack the power to grant team members formal rewards (e.g., raises, bonuses) or punishment (e.g., dismissals, demotions), team members feel less threatened exposing themselves to the consultants or confronting them. Third, because consultants are not embedded in the organizational culture, they can provide a different, more objective perspective on the team's operations. Fourth, external consultants are perceived as having greater expertise and influence than someone "in the shop." Among the disadvantages, consultants may be fairly naive about work culture compared to someone inside the organization. As outsiders, they may not really know what is going on, and therefore must spend considerable time learning about the organizational culture, the members embedded in it, and how the two interact. In light of these factors, a good consulting team may combine an external consultant with an internal one.

A consultant may assist a team building effort in several ways.

1. A consultant may help team members become aware of the group process and how it functions. Examples of process functioning include making decisions, handling conflict, taking care of task and people needs, and solving problems. The team may do this by examining issues of responsibility and accountability for implementing processes and following through on what must be done.

2. A consultant may coach or counsel team leaders and members, both within and outside team meetings.

3. A consultant may act as a referee in conflicts among team members that should be resolved outside of team meetings.

4. A consultant may discuss theory, when appropriate, to highlight or clarify team issues and problems. Examples include discussing different leadership styles and how they affect productivity and morale, or how different kinds of decision-making processes affect team involvement and commitment.

5. A consultant may reinforce (support) norms of openness and authenticity among team members. Openness includes being honest about not sharing something when an individual team members requests this. Authenticity may mean accepting the leadership style of the manager as the one most natural to that person, rather than providing a model of leadership behavior as a guide. The consultant's task would thus be to help team members deal with the manager's style instead getting the manager to behave in an "unnatural" way, and to help the manager see the consequences of her or his style.

6. A consultant may assist team members in identifying and developing their own resources and skills to complement and eventually supplant those of the consultants. The goal of consultants is to "work themselves out of their jobs"—but this is easier said than done. Usually, the consultant continues to appear periodically, albeit less frequently, for some time. This is done for at least two reasons. First, even experts have some difficulty maintaining a team building effort among themselves when they work together for an indefinite period, and this is even harder for "lay persons." Second, the effects of organizational culture—particularly its norms—on those within it will work against maintaining new behaviors deviant to the culture unless some outside influence continues to reinforce these behaviors.

7. A consultant can help team members surface their own values about work and the persons doing the work by looking for evidence of these values in their everyday behaviors. That is, consultants can help team members examine the consistency or lack of it between the values they espouse and their own behaviors (and the consequences of these behaviors). To facilitate this process, consultants can state (not advocate) their own values, which should typically reflect the consultants' concerns for the "human side of enterprise," the process by which work is done, long-term effectiveness, and continuous diagnosis.

Team building is not a one-time-only event

Any effective program dealing with interpersonal relationships and communication, developing or improving the effectiveness of work units or teams, and managing conflict and change cannot be accomplished through one or two workshops. A "one-shot" approach can actually damage an organization, stirring up issues without providing a means of resolving problems and conflicts. Moreover, such a program will make people develop expectations for improving the work situation, and they will be demoralized if no follow-up or continuing training occurs. One consequence of one-time-only events is that they leave persons far less likely to become enthusiastic or committed "the next time around." Furthermore, fulfilling an obligation to lower-level managers and employees by merely giving a program "a lick and a promise" demonstrates a lack of commitment by top management, which the rest of the organization quickly perceives.

To be effective, a team—whether it is a work unit or football team—needs the following:

- continuous, ongoing diagnoses,
- planning for and implementation of changes based on these diagnoses,
- evaluation of the changes, and
- modifications of the program as indicated by the evaluation.

Once complete, the cycle begins again. This principle is also true for relationships and working with people. Relationships are dynamic, and the persons involved in them may have difficulty effectively accommodating the demands that each situation makes of them. To assume that a one-time-only event can fully resolve team issues is extremely naive. Like a good marriage, working effectively with other people—whether they are managers or employees—is a lifetime process of learning, changing, practicing, and evaluating.

NOTE

1. Blake and Mouton (1968, pp. 97-106) found that when team members assess themselves without any structured way of doing so, they tend to base their perceptions on what they **would like** to see or believe, thus making inflated evaluations of how they operate. When, however, team members agree on an ideal model for functioning and solving problems, they thus provide themselves with a "model of excellence" against which they can measure their own behaviors. Using this model enables team members to be more objective and realistic in assessing how they are **actually** doing versus how they wish they were. Through this procedures, discrepancies become evident, suggesting starting points for team development.

REFERENCE

Blake, R. R., & Mouton, J. S. (1968). *Corporate excellence through grid organization development: A systems approach.* Houston, TX: Gulf Publishing.

BIBLIOGRAPHY

Alban, B. T., & Pollitt, I. L. (1973). Team building. In T. H. Patten (Ed.), *OD—Emerging dimensions and concepts.* Alexandria, VA: American Society for Training and Development.

Beckhard, R. (1967, March-April). The confrontation meeting. *Harvard Business Review,* pp. 149-155.

Blake, R. R., & Mouton, J. S. (1964). *The managerial grid.* Houston, TX: Gulf Publishing.

Dyer, W. G. (1977). *Team building: Issues and alternatives.* Reading, MA: Addison-Wesley.

French, W. L., & Bell, C. H., Jr. (1978). *Organization development.* Englewood Cliffs, NJ: Prentice-Hall. (See Chapter 10, "Team interventions.")

Reilly, A. J., & Jones, J. E. (1974). *The 1974 annual handbook for group facilitators.* LaJolla, CA: University Associates. (See section on team building, pp. 227-237.)

Schein, E. H. (1969). *Process consultation: Its role in organizational development.* Reading, MA: Addison-Wesley.

Developing a Productivity Team: Making Groups at Work Work

Jane Moosbruker

The initial motivation for writing this chapter came when a client said to me, "I waste so much time at the top management meetings I attend. My boss deals with us one on one. We hardly ever interact as a team, even on matters that affect all of us. I actually think he's afraid of groups." Since that time I have frequently heard variations on this theme. This chapter deals with the problems created by this situation and proposes a solution.

The introductory section demonstrates the need for a team leadership model and contrasts American and Japanese approaches to groups. The major part of the chapter presents a model group leaders can use to develop their staffs into highly productive teams. The final section provides some cautionary notes.

The need for team leadership

Today's business environment changes rapidly in financial, technological, and social arenas, resulting in greater complexity than a single individual can handle. Ideas from additional minds, specializing in different areas, are needed to stay abreast in a dynamically changing environment. Yet persons from diverse backgrounds and specialties have different perspectives on a problem. A new type of leadership is required to meld these individuals into a team that can work collaboratively toward a shared goal.

Appropriately, a renewed emphasis on leadership is occurring in today's management literature (Bradford & Cohen, 1984; Schein, 1985). A distinction is being made between "leaders" and "managers," with a leader seen as the keeper of the organization's vision, which is greatly needed in a complex, changing environment. Translating the vision into everyday management, however, requires the ability to build high-performance teams. These teams include those who report directly to a leader, as well as the cross-organizational task forces or "temporary systems" so often used to solve complex problems. The new leadership must be able to use differences in education, culture, age, and the like to enhance productivity and creativity. The most effective style for this task is one suited to the leadership of equals: a style that is low key, requiring a soft voice, a high boiling point, a talent for creating consensus, and tolerance for ambiguity (Cleveland, 1972).

Japanese organizations pay more attention to enhancing group motivation and cooperation than to motivating individual employees. Each group has a leader, but tasks are assigned to the whole group, not just to the leader, with group members responsible for deciding how to carry out the task. Firms have no job descriptions for individuals and the appraisal process evaluates the team's performance and how one cooperates with others.

In Japanese organizations, the team leader's primary function is to facilitate the group's performance. The recommended method is to create an appropriate atmosphere, a sense of identity and solidarity. Technical competence is not as important as the above qualities, and represents a potential hindrance (Hatvany & Pucik, 1981; Yoshimo, 1968).

Although emphasis on the small group may be carried too far in Japan—where evidence indicates that group goals come into conflict with corporate goals—American corporations probably pay insufficient attention to groups. In the U.S., our background and training teach us to value the individual to the point of ignoring the group. Tasks are assigned to individuals; individuals are given appraisals of their own performances. Collaboration is seldom a criteria for rewards. Often, one person will be singled out to receive an award for an achievement that required a group effort, thereby causing hard feelings among the collaborators.

The notion of the group may connote conformity, which is antithetical to our cultural heritage of rugged individualism. One may even detect the fear that relying on group decisions will lead to mediocrity because the group's competence level will sink to that of its least competent member. Research indicates, however, that group decisions are superior to individual decisions when the problem is complex (Barnlund, 1959).

In almost every organization one can hear abundant negative comments about the number of meetings people have to attend. One wonders if they are really complaining about the quantity or the quality of these meetings. When the leader lacks the skill to integrate a diverse membership into an effectively functioning team, meetings can be long, trying, and unproductive. Conformity is not what is needed, however, nor is a productive group one that conforms to the leader's or any one member's wishes. Fully productive task groups have reached a stage of differentiation at which individuals feel both a strong connection to the group and the freedom to express their own differing viewpoints in a forceful manner, trusting that they will be heard and respected.

Today's leaders need the ability to build such effective teams. Most do this on a chance basis: If it works at all, it takes a long time. The following model puts the control over building a productive team in the leader's hands.

A stage theory model of group development

Small group theorists have long believed that groups go through developmental stages (Bennis & Shepard, 1956; Schutz, 1960; Tuckman, 1965) in which major concerns or themes are paramount at different times in the group's life. "Developmental" means that the first concern must be satisfactorily resolved before the next one becomes salient. The same concept is used to describe the development of an individual personality (Freud, 1950).

Group development models may have three, four, or five stages, although they all look much alike. Each, however, "cuts the pie" a little differently.

The generalized model I find most useful (Moosbruker, 1987) is the following:

- Stage I: orientation to group and task,
- Stage II: conflict over control among the group's members and with the leader,
- Stage III: group formation and solidarity,
- Stage IV: differentiation and productivity.

These stages apply to an ongoing group. The termination of the group requires an addition to the model, and is not discussed in this chapter.

The material presented in Table 1 is meant to do three things. First, the lists of member behaviors will enable team leaders to recognize what stage a group is in. Second, the examples of frequent member concerns should help leaders understand what might be fueling these behaviors. Finally, prescriptions for leadership actions will facilitate the group's development through some difficult early stages and into productive use of its time.

For example, the behavior of a group at Stage I is uncoordinated and superficial, characterized by poor listening and many attempts to get direction from the leader. The concerns underlying this behavior are

Table 1

Stages of the Team Development Model

	Member Behaviors	Member Concerns	Leader Behaviors
Stage I: Orientation to group and task	Almost all comments directed to the leader Direction and clarification sought Status accorded to group members based on their roles outside the group Members fail to listen, resulting in non-sequitur statements Issues are discussed superficially, with much ambiguity	Who am I in this group? Who are the others? Will I be accepted? What is my role? What tasks will I have? Will I be capable? Who is the leader? Will he or she value me? Is the leader competent?	Provide structure by holding regular meetings and assisting in task and role clarification Encourage participation by all, domination by none Facilitate learning about one another's areas of expertise and preferred working modes Share all relevant information Encourage members to ask questions of you and one another
Stage II: Conflict over control among the group's members and with the leader	Attempts made to gain influence, suggestions, proposals Subgroups and coalitions form, with possible conflict among them The leader is tested and challenged (possibly covertly) Members judge and evaluate one another and the leader, resulting in ideas' being shot down Task avoidance	How much autonomy will I have? Will I have influence over others? What is my place in the pecking order? Personal level: Who do I like? Who likes me? Issues level: Do I have some support in here?	Engage in joint problem solving; have members give reasons why idea is useful and how to improve it Establish a norm supporting the expression of different viewpoints Discuss the group's decision-making process and share decision-making responsibility appropriately Encourage members to state how they feel as well as what they think when they obviously have feelings about an issue Provide group members with the resources needed to do their jobs, to the extent possible (when this is not possible, explain why)

Table 1 (cont'd.)

Stage III: Group formation and solidarity	Members, with one another's support, can disagree with the leader The group laughs together; members have fun; some jokes made at the leader's expense A sense of "we-ness" and attention to group norms is present The group feels superior to other groups in the organization Members do not challenge one another as much as the leader would like	How close should I be to the group members? Can we accomplish our tasks successfully? How do we compare to other groups? What is my relationship to the leader?	Talk openly about your own issues and concerns Have group members manage agenda items, particularly those in which you have a high stake Give and request both positive and constructive negative feedback in the group Assign challenging problems for consensus decisions (e.g. budget allocations) Delegate as much as the members are capable of handling; help them as necessary
Stage IV: Differentiation and productivity	Roles are clear and each person's contribution is distinctive Members take the initiative and accept one another's initiatives Open discussion and acceptance of differences among members in their backgrounds and modes of operation Challenging one another leads to creative problem solving Members seek feedback from one another and from the leader to improve their performances	(Concerns of earlier stages have been resolved)	Jointly set goals that are challenging Look for new opportunities to increase the group's scope Question assumptions and traditional ways of behaving Develop mechanisms for ongoing self-assessment by the group Appreciate each member's contribution Develop members to their fullest potential through task assignments and feedback

uncertainty about wanting to be in the group, fears about not being accepted by the group, a lack of knowledge about the task and one's personal competence in task areas, and uncertainty about the leader on both task and relationship dimensions. Most groups start here. Unfortunately, many groups stay here. A group may possibly get "stuck" at any of the first three stages. In what follows, I illustrate by examples some of the reasons for getting stuck at each stage. Some suggestions for facilitating the group's progress are in the text; the majority are in Table 1.

"Stuck" at Stage I

Example 1. A participative manager attempts to hold regular meetings, but they are often cancelled because key members are traveling or because higher-level personnel make conflicting demands. The meetings have no formal agenda, and no minutes are kept. Follow-up is left to the individual raising an issue. It is not clear how decisions are made, nor when a decision has been made. Task assignments are given outside the meetings and often are not discussed at the meetings. Two or three persons do most of the talking at each meeting. The problem is that the manager is not providing enough structure.

Example 2. A former U.S. Army colonel does most of the talking at his team's meetings. He passes on relevant information and shares his ideas. When he wants to hear from others he calls on them. At each meeting agenda are presented, with all of the items selected by the leader. His secretary keeps minutes and sends them out promptly. Sometimes discussion of a topic occurs, but it ends when the leader wants it to, and he makes the final decisions. This group is stuck at Stage I because it is too structured.

The major task of Stage I leadership is to provide the right amount of structure. This is not easy, because the optimum amount will vary according to the group and its members' ages, experience level, training, background, and personalities. Some members will want a lot more structure than others, and the amount they want may not be the amount the leader thinks they need.

One may, however, lead this group forward by being consistent and fair and by encouraging communication (see Table 1). But forward to what? Most group leaders find Stage II the most difficult.

"Stuck" at Stage II

Example 1. A technical manager of a decentralized operation cannot stand the bickering among her team members. She cuts off discussions when they "deteriorate into conflict." The group members usually feel relieved when this happens, doubting whether they must resolve those conflicts because they only see each other once a week. The rest of the time, the members manage similar operations in different locations. They are, however, part of a total system requiring them to use similar procedures and functions in an integrated fashion. By failing to work through differences in members' perceptions, values, and opinions with respect to these issues, the group is kept from reaching Stage III. The leader is avoiding conflict rather than facilitating conflict utilization.

Example 2. An academic department chairman runs a fairly regular and appropriately structured meeting for all faculty members. Important issues, however—such as determining who will teach how many courses and which ones—are negotiated one on one with the chairman outside the group. A great deal of competition occurs among faculty members, and a lot of hard feelings never get discussed. The group is stuck at Stage II and faced with covert conflict.

The major task of Stage II leadership is to help the group members deal with their differences with one another and, to some extent, with the leader. The "conflict" typical of this stage need not be heated. Agreements can sometimes be reached through calm and reasonable discussion, but people must feel free to raise issues concerning them (see Table 1). If the discussion becomes heated, the leader's role is to ensure that each position is heard and, as much as possible, understood. If no agreement is possible, the leader makes a decision and shares the reasoning used to reach that conclusion.

"Stuck" at Stage III

A bright, dynamic research manager who works long hours is attempting to be a participative manager. He fears that if he really shares decision-making power with his team—even though members are good at debating issues openly—performance will somehow deteriorate. His leadership style is inconsistent, as he first tries to be participative and then pulls back the reigns and makes decisions autocratically.

This manager's fear is valid in that the danger of "groupthink" is greatest at Stage III. That is, in highly cohesive groups, members may not challenge one another, but might instead overvalue one another's opinions. An "us versus them" feeling may arise, manifested in firm group boundaries and competitiveness with other groups. The leader can contribute to this situation by enhancing the group's competitiveness with or feelings of superiority over other groups.

By Stage III, group members have worked through most of their conflicts with one another, resulting in good feelings and mutual support. They may be concerned about being too close, asking themselves such questions as "Should I socialize with fellow workers?" or "How much should I talk about my personal life?"

Tension still exists concerning the leader's role, however. It may become evident in questions about how hard group members will work for this leader, how effective or "right" the group is compared to other groups and functions in the organization, or how much autonomy members actually have.

The Stage III leadership task is to trust the group members enough, and in ways that are recognizable enough to them, to enable them to feel sufficiently comfortable to challenge the leader's beliefs or decisions when they honestly question or disagree with them. If the group is really stuck in the solidarity stage, its members will not challenge one another until they can challenge the leader. The recommended leader behaviors are all excellent ways of demonstrating trust (see Table 1). Actually being challenged may not feel good. Many managers will feel like one of my clients, who—in just reading the model—said he wanted to skip this stage. The common "knee-jerk" reaction is to squelch any signs of rebellion. But only by enabling members to develop enough confidence in themselves to make jokes about their leader can a leader allow a group to function at top speed. A strong leader will not only accept this kind of pressure, but actually move the group into and through it. The following Zen saying on leadership fits this situation.

> The best leaders of all
> The people know not they exist.
> They turn to each other and say,
> "We did it ourselves."
> The next best they love and praise.

Highly competitive environments may also be responsible for groups' getting stuck in solidarity. The larger environment clearly affects what any leader can do with her or his own team. Opening up a discussion of the relevant concerns will be helpful, and may, for example, result in the members' challenging one another to achieve greater productivity while still presenting a highly unified front to those outside the group. They may even decide that they can risk modeling the kind of behavior they would like to see from the rest of the organization, such as being open and honest about both weaknesses and strengths.

I have been asked, "Is it possible and worthwhile to develop my team when my peers, boss, and boss's boss don't develop theirs?" It is possible, but more difficult. The individual leader may find this worthwhile as a skill development exercise, and it may even be successful and thus enhance the leader's career. It may be effective for the larger organization by providing a model others can follow.

Stage IV is the goal. Is there anything further to worry about? Stagnation is always a threat, which the recommended leader behaviors will help to avoid (see Table 1). Regression can also occur in group life, possibly because of a situation external to the group—such as severe financial problems in the organization—or such internal events as the loss of a member, the addition of new members, or a change in leadership. Whatever the reason, when the group regresses, the leader must revert to behaviors of previous stages, although this may sometimes feel like reinventing the wheel.

Cautionary notes

The stages in a team's development are sometimes difficult to recognize because member behaviors do not occur **exclusively** in their designated stages. One can see behaviors from all four stages at a single meeting. The majority of behaviors and the dominant theme, however, will reflect the stage the group is currently working through. One reason for the variety of behaviors is that individuals operate out of their own needs in a group, even as they are influenced by group themes. Some members may be fully collaborative from the beginning of the group's life, whereas others are distrustful or have a strong need to dominate. Members tend to become particularly active and influential as the group's major theme coincides with their own needs.

A group may also recapitulate stages at each meeting up to its current level, including floundering at the beginning, expressing conflict, resolving this and following it with joking and expressions of solidarity, and then getting down to business. This phenomenon is more pronounced when a long time elapses between meetings.

Organizational settings provide opportunities for people to meet in more than one group and to hear about one another without actually meeting. If group members have had previous experiences with one another or know one another's reputations, the group dynamics will be harder to understand and manage. A thorough utilization of the conflict typical of Stage II may require uncovering some of this data and hearsay.

Leader behaviors that can move a group forward at Stage III can cause a group to regress or get "stuck" at earlier stages. For example, the leader's being open about her or his own concerns will facilitate a Stage III group, but may frighten a Stage I group, causing its members to have less confidence in the leader. Challenging a group, which is appropriate at Stage II, may contribute to its being stuck at Stage 1 or regressing at Stage III. The reverse is less of a problem, as most Stage I and II behaviors become recognizably obsolete for the leader by States III and IV. Not that they are no longer appropriate, but they have become so much a part of the group's culture that members enact them and the leader can focus attention elsewhere. A useful rule of thumb is to do for a group whatever it cannot do for itself, and no more.

Conclusion

Bringing a face-to-face team to the productivity stage can be viewed as participative management at its most elementary level. This requires both knowledge and skill. At the earliest stage, group members are concerned with their own identity in the group; they need guidance and support. Next, they are concerned with control over themselves and influence over others; they need involvement and encouragement. They then move to concerns about closeness, competence, and pleasing one another and their leader; they need trust and self-disclosure from the leader, measured challenge, and mutually shared feedback. Finally, the group is concerned with task accomplishment. At this stage, its members need challenge and appreciation.

REFERENCES

Barnlund, D.C. (1959). A comparative study of individual majority and group judgment. *Journal of Abnormal and Social Psychology, 58,* 55-60.

Bennis, W.G., & Shepard, H.A. (1956). A theory of group development. *Human Relations, 9,* 415-437.

Bradford, D.L., & Cohen, A.R. (1984). *Managing for excellence.* New York: John Wiley & Sons.

Cleveland, H. (1972). *The future executive.* New York: Harper & Row.

Freud, S. (1950). Libidinal types. In Hogarth (Ed.), *Collected Papers.* London: Norton.

Hatvany, N., & Pucik, V. (1981, Spring). Japanese management practice and productivity. *Organizational Dynamics,* 4-21.

Moosbruker, J.B. (1987). Using a stage theory model to understand and manage transitions in group dynamics. In W.B. Reddy & C. C. Henderson, Jr. (Eds.), *Training theory and practice.* Arlington, VA: NTL Institute/University Associates.

Schein, E.H. (1985). *Organizational culture and leadership.* San Francisco: Jossey-Bass.

Schutz, W. (1960). *FIRO: A three-dimensional theory of interpersonal behavior.* New York: Holt, Rinehart & Winston.

Tuckman, B. W. (1965). Developmental sequence in small groups. *Psychological Bulletin, 63,* 384-399.

Yoshino, N.J. (1968). *Japan's managerial system: Tradition and innovation.* Cambridge, MA: MIT Press.

The Role of the Creative Outlook in Team Building

John Adams

In more than 20 years of working with teams and conducting team building sessions, I have yet to work with a team in which—initially—all the members held the same understandings about the team's core purpose or mission. Rather, in all cases team members either could not articulate the team's reason for being or held as many slightly different views about this as there were team members. Figure 1 depicts this situation, with the large arrow representing the team's purpose and the small arrows representing the team members' interpretations of the team's purpose. One may refer to this condition as a **lack of alignment**.

Obviously, in such situations much energy is expended to maintain the status quo. This energy is spent on turf battles, "just-in-case" activities, personality-based squabbles, and the like. No matter how well these symptoms of tension are resolved, they are prone to recur shortly after the team building efforts conclude. In addition, maintaining this state of tension seems to require so much energy that little remains to follow up on agreements made in the planning phases of team building, resulting frequently in eventual cynicism about the viability of team building activities. Little energy also seems available for truly making fundamental changes in the way teams operate.

Moreover, in my experience most team building efforts lead to one of two possible outcomes. One is that the team makes itself—or is made to—feel guilty about a bad situation in order to stimulate improvement. Survey feedback is often used for this purpose. The other is that the team establishes a positive goal for itself, resulting in good feelings. In both cases, however, after a few weeks or months the team reverts to its old, accustomed way of operating—having gotten over feeling either guilty or excited. Old, habitual patterns of operating and thinking reassert themselves, and "things get back to normal."

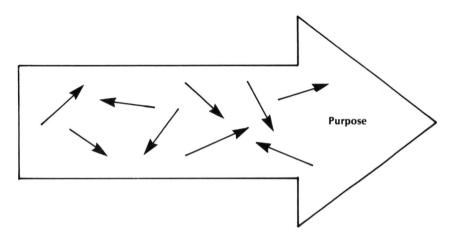

Figure 1. A typical unaligned team
(Reprinted with permission from Kiefer & Stroh (1984), *Transforming Work,* Miles River Press, p. 175)

After observing these phenomena occur in case after case over the years, I became quite curious about what naturally creates so much disalignment in teams and causes the outcomes of team building to be so transient. I also wanted to learn what I might do, in my team building efforts, to make more permanent differences in these situations.

The bases for our responses

The key to these phenomena appears to stem from how we formulate our views of reality—that is, the beliefs, attitudes, values, and expectations moderating our behavior. These fundamental "mindsets" are programmed into us during the first 10 or 12 years of our lives, quite literally by a hypnotic process. Hypnosis basically takes place when a part of one's mind—the subconscious—says "yes" to the suggestion of a person one considers an authority. When one thinks about who the authorities were for the first 10 years or so of one's life, and recalls the repeated or thematic messages sent by these authorities, the foundation premises from which one operates become obvious.

In a recent study of what children hear from adults, the investigators hung small tape recorders around the necks of young children, recording everything they heard for several days. Following a content analysis of the messages recorded, researchers learned that more than 90% of the messages parents, teachers, and other "authorities" sent children were about things the child could not do, or had done incorrectly. With such programming, no wonder we generally believe that the exter-

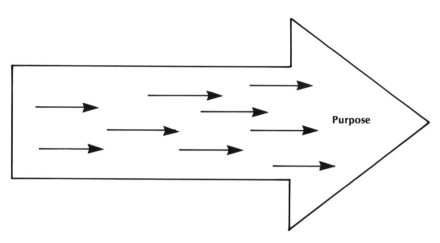

Figure 2. An aligned team
(Reprinted with permission from Kiefer & Stroh, 1984, *Transforming Work*, Miles River Press, p. 175)

nal environment controls our destinies and blame it for our shortcomings. This programming also seems to be at the root of teams' having so much trouble achieving and maintaining alignment with the teams' purposes, as portrayed in Figure 2.

I think one may safely assume that nearly all of us have been raised in such an environment, which reinforces the kind of mindset described in Table 1. We can refer to this mindset as an "operational-reactive" one, because it suggests a short-term perspective leading the individual mostly to react to stimuli from the environment.

I often find that this mindset characterizes management behavior, and even find it written into position descriptions and to be the focus of many management development programs. The basic management "functions" of organizing, directing, motivating, and controlling clearly arise from the operational-reactive mindset. Managers may be told that they are expected to "lead"—that is, to take their teams into new areas,

Table 1 The Operational-Reactive Mindset	
	Characteristics
Orientation	Maintain the status quo
Goal	Stability, consistency
Attitude toward change	Change should be slow, incremental
Time perspective	Short term, urgency
Emphasis	Problem solving, overcoming obstacles
Source of control	External environment

set examples, establish clear visions, and so forth. Looking at position descriptions or eavesdropping on annual performance reviews, however, usually discloses that operational-reactive promoting behaviors are the ones actually reinforced and rewarded by the system. Therefore, a "fire-fighting" culture emerges, and alignment occurs for only brief periods—if at all.

This mindset motto might be, "We make the best of what we have." Contrast this outlook with an alternative one, which can be called the "strategic-creative" mindset, whose motto might be "We make it up the way we want it." Another way to contrast these two outlooks is to para-phrase a statement by Robert F. Kennedy: "Some people see how things are and ask, 'Why?' Others see how things could be and ask, 'Why not?'" Only in our most inspired moments are we likely to operate from the strategic-creative mindset, as few—if any—of us have been pro-grammed to think in this way. People who are "creative," who bring forth new ideas, new art, or scientific breakthroughs have learned to operate in this way. When asked how they came up with their ideas, they respond with statements such as, "I just made them up the way I wanted them to be, and then caused them to become tangible."

The strategic-creative mindset, although unfamiliar to most of us most of the time, is a powerful stance. If a leader—or, even better, an entire team—chooses to operate from the stance of "we make it up the way we want it," incredible results become possible, as a focus on desired results replaces a focus on problems, and alignment becomes enduring as petty differences fall away.

When individuals adopt this mindset for their personal lives, clarify-ing their responses to questions such as "What is truly important in my life?" and "What do I most want to create in this situation?" alignment with the team's overall purpose or vision becomes almost automatic. People begin to see how really supporting the team's direction increases their chances of getting what is most important to them as individuals through their involvement with the team. (Of course, those who cannot put their hearts into the alignment may need to be reassigned.) But when everyone operates from a sense of what is most important to indi-viduals and to the team, the realignment process assumes much more integrity than is usually the case when "problems" are transferred to another department. Table 2 describes the strategic-creative mindset.

In summary, one can assume that most—if not all—of us have been raised in ways that reinforce our holding operational-reactive mindsets. If we are to operate on the basis of the strategic-creative mindset, we generally must explicitly choose to do so. If we do not make this choice, we are likely to spend most of our time and efforts focused on maintain-ing the status quo, preserving stability, and resisting change. We will concentrate on immediate deadlines and problems. Our experience will

Table 2 The Strategic-Creative Mindset	
	Characteristics
Orientation	To determine what I want
Goal	Alignment, empowerment
Attitude toward change	Discontinuous change is ok
Time perspective	Long term, patience
Emphasis	Focus on desired results
Source of control	Inner world

be that we are powerless to affect the forces impinging on us from the external environment.

The concept of self-fulfilling prophecy is extremely important. If I focus on problem solving, I will continue to find problems; if I focus on immediate deadlines, I will always be surrounded by immediate deadlines and experience a chronic sense of urgency; if I seek consistency and stability, I will resist any changes that are not slow and gradual. Of course, having this outlook makes it difficult to establish and maintain alignment with a clear sense of purpose, and even difficult to establish a sense of purpose at all. When longer-term plans are made and agreed to, this is done seriously, but the sense of immediacy and urgency is more powerful than the longer-term agreements. Inevitably, therefore, the plans will soon be forgotten under the pressures of meeting near-term deadlines and emergencies.

If, however, team members focus on the results they want, they will find that many of the problems "resolve themselves." If the team leader acts as the custodian of the team's vision and enables team members to align themselves, a sense of resonance can be created and tremendous amounts of focused energy will become available for high-level performance. When this happens, the team members begin to see themselves as being in charge of their own lives, and the team collectively views itself as being self-determining.

The power of this approach lies within the self-fulfilling prophecy. Remember that hypnosis occurs when one subconsciously says "yes" to suggestions from authorities. We maintain our hypnotic states with our inner dialogues—that is, with what we continually tell ourselves (posthypnotic suggestions). Thus, telling ourselves repeatedly what we want, rather than reinforcing our previous programming, subtly affects our behavior and gradually causes us to get different results. That is, **whatever you hold in your mind will tend to occur in your life**. If you continue to believe as you have always believed, you will continue to act as you have always acted. If you continue to act as you have always acted, you will continue to get what you have always gotten. If you want different results in your life or your work, all you have to do is change your mind.

How mindsets affect team building

Let us now explore more specifically the implications of these two outlooks for team building. My first point is that the predominant mindset—the one held by most of the team members—will be more powerful than any specific goals or objectives that might be articulated for the team's development. If this is the operational-reactive mindset, the team will find little good in doing long-term planning or vision building. Although one may force team members to agree with these ideals, the operational-reactive mindset will continue to reinforce a focus on immediacy and problems, and the vision or plan will fade quickly. Alternatively, if the strategic-creative mindset is encouraged, the vision or long-term goals are more easily kept in focus. The team building focus must be tied to the team members' predominant mindset, or else be specifically intended to alter it. In most cases, this means promoting a more frequent focus on the strategic-creative mindset.

Second, one must ask, "Team building for what purpose?" If the goal is to resolve long-standing issues or to concentrate on the effectiveness of day-to-day operations, then the operational-reactive mindset must predominate. If, however, the team exists in a turbulent environment, or desires to engage in strategic planning, or seeks to create a vision for itself, it must operate with a strategic-creative mindset.

With practice, team members can learn to recognize which outlook is predominant, and can choose to switch outlooks as needed. One of the most effective ways to develop this facility is to develop a list of three or four cases in which the team did not get the results it wanted, and one of three or four cases in which the team performed at optimal or inspired levels. From this inquiry should emerge, for each type of outcome, an underlying "story line." Themes and sequences of events can be identified that occur in some form in every case in which the team did not get the results desired. Different, and not necessarily opposite, themes and sequences can be identified for each case of superior performance. Further investigation should reveal that, almost universally, the mindset most in evidence when the team did not get the results it wanted was operational-reactive, and the mindset most in evidence when the team performed at superior levels was the strategic-creative.

Engaging in this same exercise on the level of the individual team member can also be revealing. Each team member will be able to identify separate story lines for inspired peak performance and for the times of poor results, which should also be strategic-creative and operational-reactive, respectively. Some teams claim they have never operated in an inspired way, and new teams have no performance records to use in this exercise. In these cases, conducting the exercise on the individual level can make the needed points adequately. Individual optimal performance themes can be pooled to describe an "ideal" team performance climate.

Another way to develop the facility of shifting between the two mindsets is to have the team members identify some things in their lives that they do not like having (e.g., bad habits, negative conditions, and the like). Ask them to identify what things they would rather have instead, stating this specifically, as if they already had them. People generally do not have much difficulty identifying the things they have and do not want, but they often have much difficulty articulating what they would like instead. This difficulty evidences how little most of us are encouraged to think in terms of what we want in our lives and work—that is, to adopt the strategic-creative mindset.

Yet another way to develop this facility is to have team members reveal to one another—in groups of three and four—those things they consider most important to themselves, the things that really matter and for which they would take a stand. In a second round, each could state what that person is most proud of in her or his work, and what each would like to accomplish in the next few years, if one's life and work could be exactly as one desires. People are surprised at how easy these sharing exercises are, and how close they feel to one another as a result of these exercises. As such, the sharing exercises both stimulate awareness about the mindset one is choosing to work from and build the team in the process.

The "new" professionals

Over the past few years, my partner, Sabina Spencer, and I have become aware of a rapidly emerging group of persons—across the spectrum of professions—who are shifting their outlooks to be more creative. We have begun referring to these persons as "the new professionals." The new professionals are managers, specialists, consultants and facilitators, educators, and others who provide the guidance, recognition, and direction their organizations need to influence the shape of our collective future.

The new professionals are persons who, after some time in their careers, find they have reached plateaus in their own development. They have become restless and eager to look deeply at the results they **are getting** and those they **could be getting** in their lives and work. They have come to recognize the significant difference between going to one's job and doing one's life work.

The new professionals want to influence how they operate with today's reality and to establish and realize powerful personal visions of the future. They are ready to meet the challenges of transforming the work place and creating environments fostering healthy and innovative approaches for living and working together. In working with these persons, my partner and I have found that they share the following characteristics:

- choosing leadership,
- being aware of underlying "automatic pilot" patterns,
- shepherding vision and purpose,
- thinking systemically,
- gaining commitment and support,
- establishing an orientation toward results.

We feel that these characteristics, although they apparently emerge naturally in many cases, must be the focus of work with teams in all types of organizations. The following paragraphs describe these six characteristics more fully.

Choosing leadership. The leadership orientation (which uses both the strategic-creative and optimal-reactive mindsets, chosen appropriately) focuses on establishing and guiding change processes, whereas the management orientation (always the operational-reactive mindset) focuses on maintaining the status quo and responding to the needs of the environment. Both are important to an organization's effectiveness, but—as noted above—most of us have been raised in the management orientation and have had little encouragement to develop the leadership orientation. Therefore, as already suggested, those who help build teams must help persons develop the facility to change from one mindset to the other.

Being aware of underlying "automatic pilot" patterns. Predictable and powerful patterns underlie both an individual's and a team's performance. To a great extent, these patterns determine what results are achieved, even though people are not usually conscious of their existence. By helping team members identify the patterns leading them to inspired levels of performance and those leading them to fail to get desired results, one can encourage both individuals and teams to establish more potent ways of operating. This allows them to transcend their negative patterns and enhance their positive ones.

Shepherding vision and purpose. Visions may be the most powerful creative forces available for leading individuals or teams to where they wish to go. They are also essential integrative mechanisms upon which team alignment depends, and necessary to the long-term effectiveness of the team's work.

Thinking systematically. Most managers now tend to accept that organizations and individuals consist of multiple interrelated and interdependent parts that coexist in an environment that itself consists of complex relationships. To have an effective influence on the future direction of a team or organization, team members must be aware of the complex web of cause-and-effect relationships in the operation of any system—including their own teams.

Gaining commitment and support. We are now finding that commitment and self-determination are of greater use to achieving sustained superior performance than are the agreement with and approval of authority, both for the individual and for teams. Team members can learn to support one another in ways that allow persons to develop and to accomplish results

Establishing an orientation toward results. Focusing on the desired results is a necessary aspect of creativity. It can prove more powerful than merely focusing on the process, efforts, or obstacles, which may bog one down. People must learn to focus simultaneously on both the current situation and on the desired results, so as to keep in mind the original goals. Teams must be encouraged to move away from an orientation toward continuous problem solving—which primarily begets more problems—and toward a results orientation, in which problems are solved along the way to realizing the desired results.

By facilitating the emergence of these six characteristics in team members, one can not only enhance the performance and fulfillment possible in effective team work, but can also enrich the team members' sense of doing their lives' work and can facilitate both the individual's and the team's capacity to become self-determining.

REFERENCE

Kiefer, C., & Stroh, P. (1984). A new paradigm for developing organizations. In J. Adams (Ed.), *Transforming work*. Alexandria, VA: Miles River Press.

Team Building at a Macro Level, or "Ben Gay" for Arthritic Organizations

Kathleen D. Dannemiller

When many of us began doing organization development work in the late 1960s, we used team building theory and practice as the foundation for our work. We defined "team building" as getting people to work together effectively toward common goals. We figured that if we could get people to do that kind of work in teams, then the organization as a whole would become more effective. Therefore, we in OD did—and still do—a lot of work on team building.

For the past several years, I have been privileged to belong to a team working under a long-term contract with the Ford Motor Company[1] to respond to a request from an executive vice president to "help our top managers become more participative . . . and do it quickly." When we began working, the automobile industry in the U.S. was declining sharply because of increased foreign competition, fuel shortages, and many years of complacency resulting from its previous ability to sell its products easily. Although regular "downturns" were expected in response to national economic cycles, this particular downturn was more severe and appeared likely to last longer than any that had occurred before. Ford's leaders urgently sought to reverse the decline by making changes both in technology and in the ways its employees worked together.

Ford's structure is what Peter Drucker (1973, p. 572) calls "federal decentralization," which occurs when "a company is organized in a number of autonomous businesses, each with responsibility for its own results, and its own contribution to the total company." Our intervention's targets were divisions within a multibusiness operation, each having several locations and plants. Each division performed the normal

---

functions required of a manufacturing organization: engineering, manufacturing, quality assurance, finance, and industrial relations.

As we began to design a large-scale intervention to respond to the request, we considered—as others had—teaching the managers of these divisions and their functions to get work done more effectively through teams, including teaching them how to deal with intergroup conflict, to run better group meetings, to identify and change group norms, and to set goals. As we observed and worked with these managers, however, we realized that traditional team building approaches for work groups would only reinforce the separation and fragmentation occurring among those performing different functions within these businesses.

The traditional functional structure works best in a stable economic environment. The environment facing Ford and other automotive companies, however, was dynamic, turbulent, and unpredictable. Old structures and developmental strategies would not work; strengthening work teams would only lead to "more of the same." Drucker also discusses the difference between efficiency and effectiveness, describing the former as "doing things right" and the latter as "doing the right things." Both efficiency and effectiveness at Ford needed attention.

Apparently, changes had to occur quickly, especially in technology (e.g., in such areas as computer-assisted design and manufacturing and in robotics). The changes our team could best focus on were improving the connections between the leaders of the separate divisions by using basic team building concepts, doing so to benefit not only the divisions, but the company as a whole.

Our work relied on three significant theories:

- Jack Gibb's team building theory of "four continuing concerns in a group" (1970),
- our adaptation of David Gleicher's change formula—D x V x F R—(Beckhard & Harris, 1977),
- our own "arthritic organization theory," which grew out of our work with Ford.

Gibb's theory

The team building theory we had been using for years with work teams stemmed from Gibb's seminal work (1970). Our version (Dannemiller, 1980) held that the three major elements of team building are (1) membership, (2) control, and (3) goal formation. Every group—new or old—has these elements in one form or another. Establishing real, shared goals requires effective communication. Clearly, if the goals are not shared, commitment to these goals is low.

These three elements usually must be addressed in the following order.

Membership. We ask the following sorts of questions when a group is in its beginning stages. Am I accepted by this group? Do I want to be part of this group? What do I have to do to be accepted? How much can I tell people about my feelings, past life, and values and still be accepted?

Control. As we begin to work on the membership issues, concerns about control begin to surface. At various times, all of us in groups ask questions such as the following: Who's in charge here? How much can I influence this group? Am I influencing it too much? Should I keep quiet or talk? Does anyone care about my area of work? Do I matter?

Goal formation. If the group has at least begun to work on the issues of membership and control, its members will begin to wonder about the group's task and ask questions similar to these: What are we here to do? Will my goals for this group be recognized? Accepted? Will we accomplish anything? Will I like it? "Buy into it"?

Gleicher's change formula

Our version of Gleicher's change formula, described by Beckhard & Harris (1977), is one we have used in our work for years as both a diagnostic and planning model. In effect, this theory holds that data about the organization and its members follows a sequence ensuring that the energy is generated to power the development process. Underlying this sequence is the formula $D \times V \times F > R$, for which the product of dissatisfaction with the present situation (D), a vision of what is possible (V), and the first steps toward reaching the vision (F) must be greater than the resistance to change (R). In our five-day participative management seminar, dissatisfaction is surfaced in the first two days. On the third day, a vision for the organization and the work groups' first steps to attain this vision are clarified. During the final two days, the organizational vision is revisited and the organization's first steps are identified and planned.

Arthritic organization theory

We developed the arthritic organization theory as we planned our work with Ford, and used this as the descriptive framework for what we did. According to this theory, the federal decentralization form of organization so prevalent in old-line businesses and industry developed from two major ideas of the 19th century and early part of the 20th century, those of Max Weber and Frederick Taylor.

Weber's work suggested that the chaos that developed in quickly enlarging organizations could be controlled by dividing responsibilities

Figure 1. "Federal decentralization"

into layers, as illustrated in Figure 1. Each layer had a clearly sensed boundary, and nothing was to "fall through the cracks." Everyone was connected, from the worker to the head of the organization.

Taylor's ideas suggested that more specification was necessary—that is, that tasks should be divided as well as responsibilities. If tasks could be separated and defined carefully—-a key feature of the "age of specialization"—work could be controlled more effectively and the organization's results predicted more easily. These concepts led to the notion of "functional chimneys" added from top to bottom to the concept of Weber's responsibility levels, as illustrated in Figure 2.

This structure seemed to work well for many years during times of stable growth. Organization development consultants—such as ourselves—spent great amounts of time working to build teams within the structure's boxes: at the top (off the job site), in the middle (doing goal setting), and on the front line (with quality of work life interventions). I considered it a great revelation to realize I had been reenforcing Taylor's principles of "scientific management" in my own work! But such work helped organizations, which grew and prospered.

Then "future shock" hit, as the environment of customers, workers, technology, and competition began to disintegrate and reform in radically different ways, requiring the organization as a whole to change how it worked, how it marketed its products, and especially what it produced and what this cost. System-wide responses were needed—quickly.

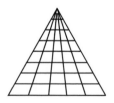

Figure 2. "Functional chimneys"

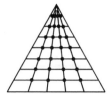

Figure 3. "Arthritic boxes"

We believed that problems in responding to this situation stemmed directly from the organizations' structure and age. Using the analogy of osteoarthritis in an aging human body, we considered these organizations arthritic, with arthritic blockages occurring at every joint. People worked out of their own narrowly defined "arthritic boxes," which occurred at all levels of the organization, across departments, divisions, and even segments of assembly lines (see Figure 3). Organization personnel had been programmed to think, "If I do my job and you do yours, the company's work will get done." Over time, those at different levels and doing different functions became so separated they often sent conflicting objectives or tasks up and down the functional chimneys. For example, if the marketing department met its goals the manufacturing department could not, or if the finance department met its goals the research and development department could not.

The task of making this total system change was expected to take five to seven years (if not longer). Recognizing this reality, as expressed by the managers at Ford themselves, we decided that rapid system-wide innovation and creative problem solving would require more than the usual team building work. It would require pulling large groups of

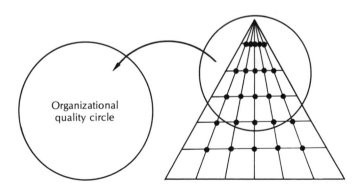

Figure 4. Organizational quality circle

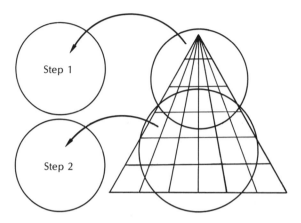

Figure 5. "Waterfall" approach

managers—in their intact work groups and functional chimneys—out of the arthritic organization temporarily by, in effect, creating an organizational quality circle, as illustrated in Figure 4. We designed a team-building intervention to occur across at least four levels of the organization, and a follow-up effort using a "waterfall" approach with middle managers by conducting the sessions twice (see Figure 5).

Implementing the concepts

Using the three theories discussed above, we planned a "generic" intervention, which actually was shaped to fit the specific "customers." Our initial effort was a five-day seminar, with participants ranging from 60-200 persons, many of whom had never been in the same room together.

We decided that the important ingredient for change was an organizational "common data base," which should be built so that the resulting cross-functional communication would help persons bypass the organization's arthritic joints. This data base included information about the following matters:

- everyone's perceptions of the organization's situation and why change was needed (dissatisfaction),
- everyone's perception of what the organization's future could be and what they preferred it to be (vision),
- which steps everyone agreed were worth taking to begin the change process (first steps).

We worked with managers from different work groups, using the team building theory (membership-control-goals) as the conceptual model for building different kinds of teams: functional teams, work teams, cross-functional/cross-level teams, and ultimately an organization-wide team, which would develop a new vision of what the organization could be and what it needed to do to get there.

We used all of the traditional team building designs, but this time at the macro level. For example, one three-hour segment was designed to deal with the organization's cross-functional arthritis (a control issue). We divided the group into functional, cross-level teams. Each team wrote to each of the other teams a note headed "These are the things you do as part of doing your job that makes our job more difficult," and signed the note with its team name. The notes were delivered by hanging them under the appropriate functional names posted on the walls of a large room. All the participants circulated around the room and read all the teams' notes. Then the teams were asked to take notes delivered to them back with them to separate breakout rooms, where they were to use the following procedure for dealing with the notes.

- **Ventilating:** Allowing time to react to the notes and to discuss what "ingrates" "they" are and how "they" don't understand "you."

- **Listening:** Following ventilation, brushing aside the feelings of resentment and rereading the notes, this time "listening" to what is said and, keeping in mind that "each group's truth is **its** truth," seeking to determine its truth about you.

- **Summarizing:** Discovering common themes among the notes.

- **Responding:** Reacting in a nondefensive way, not by telling those who wrote the notes that they are wrong or explaining to them their errors, but instead by telling them what your group is willing to do differently in response to bring the conflict to a "win-win" situation.

Each group then returned to the large room, gave its report, and sought instant feedback from all participants, or the group as a whole. (When reports were considered defensive, listeners were allowed to respond with gentle hissing.)

This macro design always produces astonishing outcomes, both for us and for the managers. A major breakthrough is achieved when one can see and hear across an old arthritic blockage, and recognize from the experience how interdependent all the company's employees must become.

Another important element of the seminar was the "preferred future" process developed by Ron Lippitt (1983), which we used to establish the system-wide goals. This was done on the third day of the seminar, when a shared data base concerning dissatisfaction and new ideas was beginning to develop. Each team was asked to develop a list of what it envisioned would happen a year later in the total system if that system were working better. The teams were also asked to list what they envisioned would happen in their own teams a year later if these teams were working effectively. All of these lists were displayed and the items listed ranked by each participant, who then made a list of the "preferred future" for the total system, citing four or five main goals. The group then developed a consensus as to the best goals for the organization. Many of the managers told us this was the first time they had experienced attempts to reach consensus at any level, especially in a large group.

Conclusion

Team building goes on, 25 years after its use began, as an important part of OD theory and practice. I know I will continue to do small group work, but the real challenge in times of transition and turbulence is to help organizations develop new ways of responding to their environments and of releasing and using the combined creativity, talent, and energy of all their personnel.

When we work with old-line organizations, we face the challenge of building a system-wide team while breaking down the old, highly structured ways so clearly defined by policies, procedures, and past practices. With newer organizations, which still reward and encourage entrepreneurs and individuality, one must work to ensure that disabling arthritis does not set in. New organizations face the danger of growth's making individualism seem—or even be—uncontrolled and uncoordinated, causing the newer organization as much trouble as the older one when adapting to a turbulent environment. Organizational team building can help both types of organizations, using different terminology and experiences, but toward the same desired outcomes: better use of talented people and more **efficient** and **effective** organizations.

NOTE

1. This team consisted of external and internal consultants. The external consultants were Alan Davenport of A.S. Davenport and Associates, Inc., Bruce Gibb of Bruce L. Gibb Associates, Inc., and my partner Charles Tyson and me of Dannemiller Tyson, Inc. The primary internal consultants were Nancy Badore, Cynthia Holm, and Jeff Walsh.

REFERENCES

Beckhard, R., & Harris, R.T. (1977). *Organizational transitions: Managing complex change.* Reading, MA: Addison-Wesley.

Dannemiller, K. (1980). *Management by objectives in higher education.* Ann Arbor: The University of Michigan Press.

Drucker, P. (1973). *Management.* New York: Harper & Row.

Gibb, J. (1970, November). *The basic reader: Readings in laboratory training.* Detroit, MI: Province V, the Episcopal Church.

Lippitt, R. (1983). Future before you plan. In R. A. Ritvo & A. G. Sargent (Eds.), *The NTL managers' handbook* (pp. 374-381). Arlington, VA: NTL Institute.

Section III.
Applications

Team Building in Voluntary Organizations

Eva Schindler-Rainman

The concept and practice of team building are familiar to persons in corporate and governmental systems. This is not true, however, in voluntary systems. The voluntary sector has seen a healthy emphasis on the importance of good professional and volunteer relationships and/or relationships between boards and staffs. Team development, building, and maintenance are becoming necessary to the survival of systems whose programs and services are delivered by a combination of paid and volunteer personnel.

A "team" may be defined as a group of persons connected by agreed-upon objectives and tasks. The team's functions may be carried out by the total group, by a subgroup, or by individuals having the support and resources of groups available to them.

Trends calling for teamwork

The team has become increasingly important because of social changes affecting voluntary organizations.

Shifting funding sources. Not-for-profit systems can no longer take for granted their dependency on traditional funding sources. New requirements of accountability, productivity, and program/service effectiveness are constantly surfacing. The world economy and the changing tax base of the U.S. affect the philanthropic dollar. Creative fund development has thus become a daily concern. To develop, inititate, and implement new funding patterns requires a unique combination of human and community resources.

It's time for a team! One system decided to recruit the following combination of persons and talents: experienced persons from the organization, persons totally new to the system, women and men representing the agency's constituencies, persons with expertise in fund raising

---

and development, and the executive director. This organization, which had depended largely on the United Way and membership funds, developed some entrepreneurial activities—such as renting space and selling goods and services—to bring in more money than previously available. This allowed the organization to increase its income from investments. The development team eventually became the finance and development committee of the board.

Moving from turfdom to collaboration. This move affects how organizations relate to one another and design collaborative programs and services. Such collaboration involves the creation of interorganizational teams to perform as planning groups, which often last into the implementation of the projects planned. For example, in one case dire need motivated many persons to realize the need for a community-wide 24-hour, seven-days-a-week emergency information and referral service. Realizing that the expertise and resources of several organizations were needed, an interagency team was developed composed of persons able to conceive and initiate the information and referral service.

The information society. Modern society now requires a much more sophisticated collection of information on wisdom, skills, and interest. Therefore, interdisciplinary teams are being formed to address such matters as restructuring an organization, analyzing its leadership, or computerizing its operations.

The world of volunteers as a visional force. The pool of volunteers available has become more multigenerational, multiculturational, multiracial, and representative of a cross section of life styles and interests. These volunteers have power and influence because they want to make a difference in the quality of life, to share their time and talent, to get personal gratification, and to help effect changes. This has resulted in the emergence of teams of staff and volunteers that are both permanent and temporary. These teams may develop personnel policies, organizational policies, or system planning. Sometimes teams are developed internally to deliver financial, public relations, or training services more effectively.

New populations. Do not overlook the identifiable, growing groups of newcomers to the U.S.; persons at risk socially, emotionally, and physically; first-offender criminals; retired citizens; those who are underemployed, unemployed, and/or receiving welfare payments; and the very young. Organizations serving these populations need their "input" through their participation in team building activities.

Positive and negative aspects of teams

Team building is a deliberate, artful action that results in a special combination of persons working with related goals, time frames, deadlines, and specific tasks. This activity can have both positive and negative aspects, as listed below.

The following are potential **positive aspects**:

- a variety of resources becomes available,
- participants become willing to undergo training and grow together,
- persons from different parts of an organization can work together on a project,
- persons from both within and outside an organization can participate,
- persons become exposed to opportunities to be leaders and followers,
- new investment in the organization's mission may be developed,
- persons may have the chance to meet personal needs for interaction and support,
- team members can belong to something bigger than themselves,
- volunteers and paid personnel can work together for a common cause,
- persons get the opportunity to work on a project with a deadline, finish the project, get rewarded for their efforts, and celebrate,
- persons can experience the special camaraderie associated with belonging to a successful, productive team,
- top management lends its support.

The following are potential **negative aspects:**

- team members' commitments may be incompatible,
- team members may have hidden agenda that interfere with the process,
- the process may suffer from poor work or a lack of follow-through,
- someone may be unable to work as a group member,
- the team may lack clear direction or a sense of purpose,
- the leaders may have a laissez faire attitude,
- staff-volunteer practices, roles, and/or relationships may not be satisfactory,
- one may lose one's perspective on the job's importance,
- organizational inexperience may hinder the process,
- the organization may not support the team as it should,

- meetings may suffer from inconsistent attendance,
- delegations may suffer from poor performance,
- unappreciated and unsupported teams often disintegrate.

Strategies for composing voluntary system teams

Both the size and "texture" of voluntary system teams vary tremendously. Such teams may consist entirely of persons inside an organization, or they may be combinations of internal and external personnel. Teams may exist on an ongoing basis—such as professional office teams that meet weekly to determine how support services are to be provided-and develop reciprocal feedback systems to maintain quality. Sometimes teams are temporary systems to produce specific services, programs, or ideas. Teams may consist of representatives of specific locations, functions, or places in the hierarchy, or they may be combinations of providers and consumers of services.

In **structuring and developing** a voluntary system group that one hopes will become a team, one should seek to meet the following criteria:

- clear, "do-able" goals or desired outcomes,
- making certain that those to be affected by the team's work are represented on the team,
- restricting the number of team members to 3-13 individuals, because if the number is too large or too small cohesiveness is difficult,
- recognizing the beauty of differences, for a team should be able to produce a better program, product, idea, or service than any member could produce alone,
- sharing various experiences to enrich the team's resources,
- developing orientation and training activities,
- giving thoughtful consideration to recruiting and placing team members,
- possibly developing contracts between team members and between the team and the system, instituting regular procedures for stopping proceedings, and giving/receiving feedback within the team and between the team and the system,
- providing recognition, visibility, and celebration and reward procedures, as these are vital to team life,
- deciding how long the team will exist—even if this decision is changed later—so as to help team recruiting, building expectations for the team, and maintaining the team.

Efforts to **maintain team morale** and motivation should include the following:

- scheduling progress reports and celebrations,
- exchanging ongoing feedback,
- supporting the team as an integral part of the total organization, as well-functioning, cohesive teams sometimes become entities exclusive of others,
- designing an open-ended recruiting policy to enable team members to come and go by design,
- carefully documenting the process and product(s) of the team's work,
- considering shared, functional, temporary, or other leadership patterns making leadership opportunities available to more than one team member,
- providing ongoing support structures and staff services,
- making sure lines of communication to and from the team are clear,
- offering ongoing team training as the organization changes,
- agreeing on regular meeting times and suitable meeting places,
- acknowledging and recognizing team members as appropriate.

Conclusion

Combining diverse human resources is what team building and maintenance are all about. Voluntary systems need to reorient their thinking, ways of working, and structure to accommodate and encourage a variety of teams to do the work that one or two persons—or committees—usually did in the past.

BIBLIOGRAPHY

Greenleaf, R. (1977). *Servant leadership.* New York: Paulist Press.

Hardy, J. (1984). *Managing for impact in nonprofit organizations.* Erwin, TN: Essex Press.

Kanter, R.M. (1983) *The change masters.* New York: Simon and Schuster.

Schindler-Rainman, E., & Lippitt, R. (1980). *Building the collaborative community.* Riverside, CA: University of California Extension.

Schindler-Rainman, E., & Lippitt, R. (1973). *Teams training for community change: Concepts, goals, strategies and skills* (2nd ed.). Riverside, CA: University of California Extension.

Working with Teams in the Public and Business Sectors: Ways of Dealing with Major Differences

Robert T. Golembiewski

Some wag once wrote that public management and business management are alike in all unimportant ways. Although I do not fully accept that characterization, it helps introduce my discussion of the seven important ways in which I have found that business and governmental settings **tend to differ**.

The usual cautions apply, for readers should not be surprised if any two public and business organization are actually quite similar. For example, some businesses have world-class quantities of the very qualities considered endemic to public agencies, and government agencies such as the Passport Office of the U.S. Department of State have production records that are second to none. Therefore, I focus on probabilities. Probabilities can never replace detailed diagnoses of specific sites, however. This discussion of definite differential tendencies may thus help consultants ask correct questions, but will poorly serve those seeking absolutes when probabilities are intended.

Specifically, seven themes are addressed. In turn, these themes deal with differences between public and business organizations related to

- the dominant emotional mode,
- the frequency of crises of agreement,
- the prevalence of loose coupling,
- the ubiquity of power and of love/trust,
- the operating approach to confidentiality,
- the special role of ''losers,'' as variously defined, and

- the special function of the press.

Some general notes expand on the seven themes, and discussion of each includes one or more "implications," which guide the consultant working with public-sector teams. Note that this overview relates most directly to the "interface" of politics and administration, which I have often worked with. In this interface political appointees associate with top-ranked permanent bureaucrats, and it constitutes a kind of fault line on which public and private interests play out their most consequential pushing and shoving over who gets what—and where, when, and how.

1. Fear and the slough of despond

In my experience, at the interface of politics and administration the featured emotional tone is fear, often a despondency that "it's bigger than any—or all—of us." Those in business know fear, too, of course, but not so continuously and persistently as those at this interface in public organizations. Curiously, compared to most of their business counterparts, those in the public sector find that this emotion worsens as they approach the top. As one indication of this, consider the results of a survey of a substantial number of executives. Of those in business, more than 80% would advise their children or young friends to pursue careers like their own. Among government executives, about the same proportion would advise the opposite (Schmidt & Posner, 1987).

I will not try to defend the adequacy of this description, but will share what I try to do as a consultant when the reality I face has the features I consider common at the interface. These implications seem profound to me, although I only rely on two in this chapter to illustrate the far-longer catalog.

Implication I. The central issue at the interface can be dealing with feelings of helplessness or hopelessness. In sharp contrast, most of the OD literature gives primacy to inducing valid and reliable information, along with building processes and norms adequate for sustaining the flow of high-quality data. These practices are important, but they often do **not** relate to the primary need at the interface.

Given the attractiveness of generating valid, reliable information—and the useful technology for doing so via various interaction-centered designs—the key issues at the interface stem from outcomes that are common **even when** high-quality information is both available and shared. In short, actors do not see how they can respond to what they know while still maintaining enough support from the constituencies keeping them in valued spots. To say somewhat the same thing, the political zeitgeist often is so robust that politicos respond to it even as they acknowledge the strangeness of doing so. Consider the case of Muskie's 1972 primary campaign in New Hampshire: He "lost" even though he actually won the primary, because his margin was not considered "big enough," and he thus developed the image of loser even while winning. This image persisted even though New Hampshire had only about 100,000 Democratic voters and Muskie shortly thereafter won the primary in Illinois, a state with 10 to 15 times as many Democratic voters as New Hampshire.

Implication II. Public-sector interveners often need to give as much or more attention to making information "palatable"—politically acceptable—as they do to generating the information. This often involves the **"person"** of the intervenor, who becomes seen as a risk taker or "point man," or as an idea generator or catalyst who can suggest or stimulate politically acceptable ways of acting on available data. Both alternatives imply an active, broad role for the intervenor in the face of obvious dangers.

2. Frequent crises of agreement

Related to the above, I find a high frequency of "agreement" at the politics/administration interface. The situation resembles that of Janis's "groupthink" and Harvey's "Abilene paradox." That is, the attractions of membership in high-level public-sector teams can be so great that individuals fear being the only ones to deviate from the group's opinion. They may see themselves as the only deviants, when actually many—or even all—of the other members also disagree but will not admit this publicly. The "group opinion" may thus exist only because no one will disavow it. The fear of losing valued membership dominates, and it can be so substantial that it paralyzes people.

Most OD designs address disagreement or conflict, with the dominant issue considered to be fear of "unsatisfactory inclusion"—a "we versus they" situation. Such situations seem amenable to easy improvement by various confrontational designs, the sharing of three-dimensional images, or other methods. People often have little to lose in these cases, and sharing even painful information can help build bridges across previously troubled waters. Such designs appropriate for situations of "disagreement," however, can be awkward for use in the "agreement" situation of the politics/administration interface—even counterproductive. Valid, reliable data can be liberating when conflict is present, but when awkward agreement exists the same kind of data tend to make matters **worse** by threatening the very membership whose attractiveness had caused withholding. Even if that great obstacle is overcome, others remain. People will fear, "If we are so great, how could we do such a silly thing? And what defense do we have against its happening again?"

Implication III. In all cases, but especially at the politics/
administration interface, diagnose for agreement or disagreement.
When in doubt, intervene as if a crisis of agreement exists. Being wrong
will only make clients wonder why you are proceeding slowly and cau-
tiously. If you mistakenly intervene as if the crisis is one of disagreement, however, the prognosis has some wicked features: The greater the
intervention's impact, the higher the probability of reinforcing the crisis
of agreement. Fortunately, convenient diagnostic tools exist for indicating whether agreement or disagreement exists.

Furthermore, useful designs for the two conditions seem reasonably
distinct, given an almost lack of research (Golembiewski, 1979).

3. Prevalence of loose coupling

The sense of loose versus tight coupling is widely appreciated, so a brief
description here should suffice. Generally, loosely coupled systems are
characterized by unclear and overlapping sources of authority, uncertainty about roles and priorities, and the like. Table 1 presents the major
features of what will henceforth be called "overbounded" and "underbounded" systems.

Despite common conceptual appreciation of differences between
the types of systems, their implications for designs are too frequently
overlooked. The common culprit is the bias toward interaction-centered
designs, which stems from a belief in the often-commendable notion
that real progress requires the prior creation of appropriate cultures at
work. Overbounded systems may respond well to interaction-centered
designs, as these can "free" individuals who are constrained and
repressed. The same prescription could have disingenuous results for
underbounded systems, however, and might prove seriously counterproductive. Systems diagnosed as underbounded may well require other
types of designs, such as basic structural interventions designed to
"stiffen" their loose features.

Implication IV. Think first of the interface as loosely bounded or
underbounded. You will often be correct. Even if you are wrong, your
perception will be less harmful than one leading you to intervene mistakenly as if the system were tightly bounded or overbounded.

Implication V. Do not decide quickly in favor of interaction-centered
designs. For example, simple role negotiation or role analysis designs
may help reduce the probabilities of things falling "through the cracks"
or of conflicts developing over jurisdiction. Both are likely in underbounded systems. Basic structural revision may also be relied on, as
relevant success stories attest (Carew, Carter, Gamache, Hardiman,
Jackson, & Parisi, 1977). Or, if the system is highly autocratic and contains little of the attitudes and/or skills required by interaction-centered

Table 1
Features of Overbounded and Underbounded Systems

	Overbounded systems	Underbounded systems
System characteristics		
Authority relations	Well-defined hierarchy and authority for decision making	Unclear authority sources and overlapping authority
Role definition	Overly specified and constraining roles Strictly defined jobs	Uncertainty about limits of priorities or roles
Management of human energy	Difficult to release energy Resources are dammed up and blocked	Difficult to harness energy Resources are physically and emotionally dispersed
Communication	Easy to convene groups Problems with distortion and invalid information	Difficult to promote communication Absence of communication
Affect	Egocentric Ethnocentric Suppression of (strong) emotions	Negative internal and external emotions
Economic conditions	Stable and wealthy	Uncertainty about sources of funding Money is "tight"
Time frame	Relative long-term security Loss of responsiveness to change	Survival and crisis orientation

designs, the intervenor might begin with such gentler—but often effective—designs as flexible work hours, which will help develop confidence in the participative systems that interaction-centered designs have as their goal.

Urging apt diagnosis and appropriate prescription is easier said than done, of course. Some things can never be repeated too often, however, to ensure that no one will forget they are true, even if difficult. This is particularly so when the usual bias toward interaction-centered designs may result in their awkwardly fitting an extant condition—such as the underbounded system I see as more likely in the politics/administration interface.

4. Dealing directly and constructively with power phenomena

All organizations have as priorities the gaining and maintaining of power, but I have never found this to be as persistent and insistent as at the politics/administration interface. This may bother consultants nurtured on the "truth-love" model, but that is **their** problem. At this interface the major problem is getting and keeping power, and consultants must respect this if they are to affect such systems in ways consistent with the values of OD. How can a consultant respond to such situations constructively and with integrity to OD values? The following discussion of several implications may help, but the job will never be easy or without cross-pressures.

Implication VI. Even apparently superficial interventions can have political effects, nowhere more so than at the politics/administration interface, where everything is or may be political. Hence, a consultant who proposes to be merely facilitative will provoke incredulity. From this system's perspective, the consultant operating from the base of OD values almost always represents an alternative approach to gaining and maintaining power. Circumlocution will only impress the unwary, and even then only temporarily.

Implication VII. By several orders of magnitude, I find the demand for "silent servant" consulting to be greater in the public sector than anywhere else. Silent servants isolate and ratify only that wisdom acceptable to some establishment, or they only legitimate what that establishment would like to say but considers impolitic—even dangerous—to enunciate.

Surely the practice of OD involves some degree of silent servant consulting, and practical considerations can generate powerful motivations to play along. I try to resist that temptation, resolving most issues in doubt by assuming that a contract process with a high "fog quotient" is probably a test of my willingness to be a silent servant.

5. A relaxed approach to confidentiality

At times confidentiality is required, but I find it useful at the politics/administration interface to insist on the following:

> We can signal confidential elements, but in general I can be most helpful when you rely on my discretion about using materials. Generally, I will disguise sources, and I will try to check with you beforehand if I have even a minor doubt about the probity of any

disclosures. But sometimes neither will be possible. I hope, as our relationship matures, that I will earn a longer and longer leash.

Too often for my comfort, I find that insistence on confidentiality has two effects at the interface. One is that the consultant may be keeping something confidential that is actually known to various other persons. Second, the person seeking confidentiality from the consultant may be doing so for the purpose of testing the consultant's fidelity, or of hamstringing the consultant with information that cannot be verified or used but that nonetheless encumbers the intervenor and even makes that person timid. One may test fidelity more directly than by laying traps dealing with absolute confidentiality, and I try to avoid the latter situation altogether.

Implication IX. Ask yourself and the person requesting confidentiality, "Is confidence really necessary in this case? What is the purpose of someone's sharing something confidential with you while asking you to withhold it from others?"

Team-oriented designs offer the advantage of limiting the need for "confidentiality games" within the team. Such games also exist for use at the interteam level, too, of course—and this advice is also applicable for those situations.

6. The interface abhors "losers"

Consider two scenarios that hold true in most organizations, but nowhere more so—in my experience—than in the public sector. First, the tension between those with high status and those with low status is a central dynamic of organizational life. Second, failure is usually an orphan, but success typically has numerous parents.

What does this imply for consulting with public-sector teams, especially at the politics/administration interface? The five implications below suggest the broader range; the full story is beyond the scope of this chapter. The following discussion, however, reflects adaptations appropriate for the common, great public-sector sensitivity to so-called losers and losing.

Implication X. Many interaction-centered designs have the effect of giving a new voice to various organizational "losers." Thus, they give critics of a team's leadership a legitimate opportunity to complain via a confrontation design or the sharing of images, and a member currently in the "deep freeze" may be given a chance to voice displeasure or even to discourse on the injustice of it all.

No leaders enjoy such occasions, but leaders in the public sector enjoy them less than anyone else. I can only guess as to why this is so, (see Golembiewski, 1985, pp. 237-245, for a detailed discussion), but hypothesize that the pecking order in the public sector may be both more important and more unstable than that in many business settings. This is consistent with the observed loosely coupled character of much of the public sector.

Implication XI. Consultants should be careful about designs that let people "blow off steam," which are common to team building efforts. The danger is particularly great when the concern basically derives from policies or structures imposed by some distant authority, such as a legislature. Under such conditions, designs emphasizing venting can make everyone a loser. Through processes of "resonance," they may paradoxically heighten despair and even conformity to general opinions of being stuck, which may be reinforced or even revealed by the designs themselves.

Implication XII. Some clients get the idea that team building can provide the impetus for eliminating individuals, even determined "losers" who for various reasons have maintained their membership even though they have lost standing. In such cases, teams can assume the character of a firing squad, acting on behalf of manipulative managers.

This point should also occur to consultants. Early in the contract process, prudent consultants should seek to reduce the possibility that any team design will be used in such a direct, instrumental way. Avoid being some else's "hit man." Separation for cause ideally should precede team building rather than follow it. In short, aggressively probe to uncover any "walking wounded." A manager with insufficient resources and determination to eliminate an irritating employee is not likely to generate or profit from an effective team building experience.

Implication XIII. Seek consulting conditions that reduce the probability of failure (for the characteristics of a favorable case, see Kiel, 1982). In general, an intervention with a low probability of success is even riskier in the public sector. Remember two points. First, the public sector likes "winners," in consulting as much as anything else. Second, the most powerful single intervention a consultant can make is to say, "I don't believe it would be prudent to go ahead with this, at least not at this time."

Implication XIV. Set realistic, limited learning goals and use multiphase designs that build on one another but can be interrupted if the political winds change, as they inevitably will. Success rates in public-sector OD seem substantial, only slightly less than those for business settings (Golembiewski, 1985, pp. 43-130). But no one needs to risk being branded a loser by advertising comprehensive programs for cultural change that, for various reasons, probably will not be completed in one fell swoop. Instead, think of multiple stages that all lead to such change, but which can be independently packaged and assessed for progress toward OD goals before the cosmic vision is achieved, if that ever occurs.

7. The press holds all the trump cards

The consultant working with public-sector teams may have to deal with the press, especially at the politics/administration interface. This is putting it mildly. I have undergone nothing in the business sector equivalent to the journalistic fire storms of opinion that have accompanied several public-sector interventions. I have never even received a news media request—much less a demand—to be present at a business team building session. Such demands by the press are quite common in public-sector consultation, however, apparently based on the general principle that no one can own 51% of the stock in a public agency.

Politics and administration can be viewed as sort of tectonics plates whose bumping and grinding attract both consultants and journalists. Even though business meetings are also the target of profound public interest, consultants involved in them get relatively little or no attention from the press. Public sector consultants and the news media constitute a kind of odd couple, as the following discussion suggests.

Implication XV. The press holds all the trump cards for public-sector consulting, **as it should**. One major way—sometimes the only practical way—to create a sense that something is "everybody's business" is via the news media. Therefore, the public-sector consultant needs a sense of priorities. The team one works with is important, but the public clearly has a right to know what is happening. One hopes that team can build its own case to present to its constituents, but the press may and often should be present. In states with "sunshine" laws requiring open meetings, the public-sector team has no choice in this, although matters related to personnel and real estate often are considered privileged.

Implication XVI. The news media's interests and the "truth" according to management may seldom coincide, but having a team and consultant act in secret can only worsen matters. In an extreme case, local television news programs broadcast the team building sessions of a city management group. In another, reporters attended team building sessions and were shuttled out of the room when private issues were discussed.

This may complicate the consultant's work, even under the best of circumstances. In the worst situation, would-be news media stars can distort and exaggerate reality to "get a story." This system may seem awkward, but it is the best one we have.

Postscript

This chapter discusses seven areas in which businesses and public-sector organizations generally exhibit major differences, and presents implications of these differences for consultants working with teams. Those readers seeking to read more about this may wish to consult my book on the topic (Golembiewski, 1985).

REFERENCES

Carew, D. K., Carter, S. I., Gamache, J. M., Hardiman, R., Jackson, B. W., III, & Parisi, E. M. (1977). New York State Division for Youth: A collaborative approach to the implementation of structural change in a public bureaucracy. *Journal of Applied Behavioral Science, 13*(3), 327-339.

Golembiewski, R. T. (1979). *Approaches to planned change* (Vol. 2). New York: Marcel Dekker.

Golembiewski, R. T.(1985). *Humanizing public organizations: Perspectives on doing better than average when average ain't at all bad.* Mt. Airy, MD: Lomond Publications.

Kiel, D. H. (1982, December). Impact of the first three years of the North Carolina Governor's Program for Executive and Organization Development. *Public Administration Review,* pp. 375-383.

Schmidt, W.H., & Posner, B. Z. (1987, September). Values and expectations of city managers in California. *Public Administration Review,* pp. 404-409.

Section IV.
Clients and Consultants

For the Manager Who Must Build a Team

Judith D. Palmer

The first thing to keep in mind is this: "Don't panic!" The concept of team building may seem intimidating, the province of experts and consultants. So you must remember that you are already a manager; that you have some experiences and successes to draw upon; that you have some ideas of what kind of team you want to develop. The information in this book has some excellent ideas that can guide you, but you are the one who is going to build a team—and you can do it.

Much of the team building process can be done **only** by the manager and the other persons involved in the everyday activities for which the team has been formed. A team building specialist can help you with some of this process and can conduct specific events for you, thus freeing you to act as an individual rather than from your hierarchical position. But nothing can replace the hands-on, daily influence you will have in determining your team's climate, norms, and results.

What is team building, anyway? It is a **process** that evolves over the life of a team. The process can be helped through the setting aside of time for certain **events** called "team building meetings," but it would be unrealistic to think that any given event can "do it" for the team. Your guidance, and a sustained effort toward realizing your vision of the team as a working unit, are what makes team building happen. This chapter provides some models and guidelines for your use. These include creating your own vision, four stages of team development, the "basic triangle" of team organization, and some specific actions you can take to build your team.

Creating your own vision

First, take stock of the situation. Read the following questions; as you answer them mentally, you may benefit from taking notes. Read slowly and let your mind rove. Consider not only the actual answers, but other thoughts that occur to you as you go along.

1. Is this team newly formed, or has it existed for some time?
2. Do most of the members know one another?
3. Are you new to them as their manager? Have you worked with them before?
4. Will the team be disbanded after it does a specific task, or will it last for a long time and do successive tasks?
5. Do the team members need to cooperate and rely on one another, or just do their jobs?
6. Do the members know how to do this job? Have most of them done it before?
7. Does the team have problems within it that must be addressed?
8. What is your vision or ideal of how the team should be?

The last question is particularly important. You will find it helpful to spend some time imagining what you really want the team to be like, how it will solve problems, how it will address its task, how its members will interact, and how you as the leader will relate to the members individually and as a team. Sit back, close your eyes, and in your mind "run a movie" depicting how you want the team to be.

The outcome of good, ongoing team building should closely resemble your ideal, and this chapter will help you start in the right direction. To be fair, I should share with you my own "mental movie" forming the basis of this chapter, as it may not fit your own concept of the ideal team.

The ideal team I envisioned in writing this chapter is one whose members know and trust one another's abilities, are aware of one another's shortcomings, and "back up" one another. The team is organized to do its task, and it proceeds at a pace that is energetic but does not cause people to burn out. Progress is measured against concrete milestones, but no one is afraid to "blow the whistle" if the schedule and deadlines are forcing the team to make improper decisions along the way. The team's leader is considered fair and supportive, and is acknowledged by the members as the one who can make final judgments, negotiate with upper management, and set direction for the team as necessary. Conflicts are aired and resolved in a straightforward manner. The climate is one of energy and enthusiasm; members feel a sense of urgency and dedication to the task, and they keep one another on track. The members appreciate and enjoy one another for who they are.

Four stages of a team's development

A team is a living entity. Like any organism, each team evolves from early to mature stages, independent of the nature of the team or the task it must perform (for a fuller discussion of the concept of group development, see the *Reading Book for Human Relations Training*, Porter & Mohr, 1982). One aspect of this development is the members' attitudes or relationships, both within the team and with you, the team leader. You may find it helpful to monitor and assist the progress of your group's evolution by keeping in mind the following concise "formula" describing the four stages of team's development: "forming, storming, norming, and performing."

Forming. While it is forming, a team is not sure what its task is. Its members do not know one another well, nor have they learned what sort of leader they have. They tend to be obedient, to want to be told what to do, and to express any negative feelings either politely or privately.

During this stage, your role as a leader is to empower the members and to assist them in establishing solid guidelines for proceeding to perform the task. Yes, you should offer guidance and set directions for the task—but you should also ask members their opinions and act on them when you can, and acknowledge areas in which you are not an expert or lack experience. Solicit the group's views by asking open-ended questions instead of those requiring only "yes" or "no" answers. Compliment the members when appropriate. These and other gestures of respect and encouragement will help you temper your "boss" role and make members more willing to contribute their ideas.

Storming. In this stage, group members feel more comfortable expressing their opinions. They begin to explore how much power they can wield and to test the manager's limits. Arguments, misgivings, counterproposals, and a general increase in the level of frustration are indicators of this stage. Challenges often arise not only concerning what the team must do and how to do it, but also concerning the leader's role and style of leading the effort. As the leader, you must understand that this phase is healthy—and that you cannot avoid it. A team that does not go through the storming phase will not learn to deal with conflict. Such teams are capable of "malicious obedience"—that is, of doing what the leader says, even when the members know that it is not the right thing to do. Teams that never "storm" are passive, fragmented, and significantly less creative.

Your role is to help your team through this stage by dealing directly with conflict in the best ways you know. Some helpful ways of handling conflict in this stage include the following: remaining objective, even when the target of the hostility is you or your ideas; calling in a neutral third party to manage the discussion of "hot" issues; helping the group clarify the nature of the conflict; and calling on members' skills to help resolve it. You should also find it helpful to set up operating principles and procedures to provide criteria for resolving some arguments. Finally, keep reminding yourself not to take conflict too personally.

Norming. This stage results from what was learned in the previous stage. Based on its cumulative experience, the team begins to establish procedures for handling decisions, crises, conflicts, and approaches to the task. Even in the most formal organizations, teams develop their own ways of doing things as members weather storms with one another and begin to build trust. Leadership emerges among the team members, and the leader begins to feel less like a referee—or punching bag—and more like the leader or manager he or she envisioned being.

Your best course during this stage and the one that follows is to continue the activities that create trust, empower team members, provide a vision of the team functioning at its optimum, and help build skills in decision making and conflict management. As the leader, you will still have responsibility for ensuring that priorities are set and followed, and you will be the ultimate tie breaker, but the group increasingly does more of this for itself.

Performing. This stage is the payoff for going through the three previous stages. The team has learned how to be a team, has defined its tasks, has worked out its relationships, and has aligned itself toward producing results.

Your role at this stage calls for vigilance. First, congratulate yourself for guiding the team this far. Continue to be alert, however, to the team's needs for further improvement in skills and attitudes. Like a living organism, the team will react to influences inside or outside its boundaries, such as changes in its task, its membership, or its environment. It may need anything from "fine tuning" to returning to "square one." Indeed, teams often go through this four-stage cycle several times. This model can be a helpful "road map" for you to use in judging where the team is with respect to its development, where it is heading, and what you can do to keep it moving toward maturity.

The basic triangle

The four-stage model describes how team members learn to interact. But you must still address the job the team has been asked to perform. You must therefore clearly establish the structural elements that provide the foundation for a well-working, smooth operation, enabling the team to make progress toward attaining its goals. Figure 1 below shows the "basic triangle" of key elements necessary for the team to do its job. The elements are **the task, the team,** and **the tools.** Together they

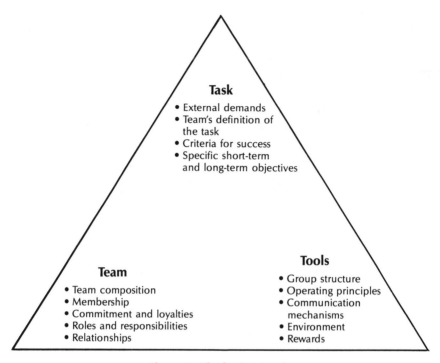

Figure 1. The basic triangle

form a solid foundation for the team to build on; remember, the tripod is one of the most stable support bases. As the leader, your responsibility is to help the team keep the key elements in balance, because any given team will consider one or some of the elements to be more important than the others.

Angle 1: The task

A team's task must be defined in a way that enables all the members to know exactly what they are to accomplish, and minimizes the amount of time spent on unfocused, off-target efforts. You must help the team understand the task in ways that will guarantee success, including by explicitly discussing and understanding the following four factors:

- stakeholders and external demands,
- the team's definition of the task,
- criteria for success,
- specific short-term and long-term objectives.

Stakeholders and external demands. Nothing is as demoralizing as brilliantly executing a task, then finding out that the result was not what the person making the request really wanted. A team's assignment typically is given by someone outside the team, such as a client or higher-level manager, meaning that the team itself is not the first to define the task. Therefore, it is important to analyze the assignment and understand the needs and goals, both expressed and unexpressed. The team should determine who the "stakeholders" are—that is, the persons and organizations whose needs must be satisfied by the team's results—and what they really want.

For example, if the team is assigned to build a better mousetrap, it must determine if the real need is to (1) catch mice or (2) keep mice out of a house. Crafting a beautiful, stainless steel mousetrap will not suffice if the real need is for people in a household never to see a mouse, nor will designing a new, absolutely mouse-proof house if the client (or manager or stakeholder) wants results within two weeks. You must help the team both understand and challenge the expressed needs of the stakeholders. Furthermore, you must recognize that the stakeholders do not always know what they really want. This calls for creativity and expertise, so that ideally the end result will be even better and closer to the stakeholders' real needs than what was initially requested.

Definition. A truly excellent team does not always restrict itself to executing the assignment as given. In redefining a task, the team should also address its own needs, goals, feelings, and values. When asked, for instance, to build a better mousetrap, a team might define its job as designing a system for keeping a house free of mice while still respecting the sanctity of all life and providing separate but safe environments for both humans and other living creatures. This would go beyond—but not compromise—the assignment originally given the team, and could include improvements that would inspire commitment and enthusiasm from team members. The team must also add much operational detail, scheduling, and the like to its own definition of the task.

Criteria for success and short-term and long-term objectives. Determining how to measure achievement is extremely important. This involves establishing criteria for success (e.g., customer satisfaction, low cost, appropriate timing)—including who must agree the job was done successfully—and short-term and long-term objectives that indicate milestones toward completion of the assignment.

You should help the team address these elements in defining its task so that the group can harness its energy and align itself for success. This is often not considered part of "team building," but it is essential to building your team. One way to clarify the task is to establish a procedure or set up a series of meetings devoted entirely to task definition. The format can be as simple or complex as you wish, but it should basically consist of four steps, each of which you, the manager, can conduct.

Step 1. Have the primary stakeholder (i.e., manager or client) speak to the team, or else make a presentation yourself, defining for the team what it is requested to do. Be as specific as possible. Encourage all team members to question, challenge, and explore the implications. This step is best done separately from the next one, thus giving team members time to think about what was said.

Step 2. Present the four factors associated with the task, listing them on a flip chart or blackboard. Explain why all four are important to the group's understanding of its mission. Go over each one in "brainstorm" fashion, asking for everyone's comments, questions, and suggestions. Write down everything that is said; do not edit, interpret, or consolidate anything; allow the ideas to flow, and capture each one. In discussing **stakeholders and external demands,** learn the team's understanding of the assignment as given and probe for other external demands; list them all, and make a separate list of unanswered questions. For the **team's definition of the task,** have members discuss how they want to add to the definition and what values and approaches they consider central to accomplishing the assignment (you may wish to hold a separate meeting on this topic, with an expert helping the group articulate its vision of the desired outcome). Address **criteria for success** by creating lists in a brainstorm fashion, again keeping track of unanswered questions. Finally, discuss **short-term and long-term objectives** by seeking the group's best judgment and acknowledging "givens."

Step 3. Assign individuals or subgroups, preferably on a volunteer basis, to prepare and present to the group draft versions of the following:

- a proposed "mission statement" for the team,
- a list of the external demands, both those expressed and those interpreted by the team,
- a list of the criteria for success and a list of the persons who must agree the task was done successfully,
- short-term and long-term objectives.

Step 4. Have the whole team meet again to review and agree on the items related to the four factors. Make as many revisions as necessary to ensure that the team can give its "informed consent" to the definition of the task.

Review the decisions arising from this process on a regular basis so that you can be certain they continue to be relevant, and so that new team members can be informed of and agree to them.

Angle 2: The team

Developing the team's internal process is the usual focus of team building. Many good articles have been published on this topic, and experts are available to help you with some of the specialized aspects of team building. As the team's leader, you should have an overview of what its development includes, as much of the responsibility for making it happen is yours. The major factors affecting the team are

- team composition,
- membership,
- commitment and loyalties,
- roles and responsibilities,
- relationships.

Team composition. This issue can only be resolved after the team's task has been clarified. What sorts of skills and experience are needed to do the job? Often, a team is formed before it is fully understood what sorts of people are required, and thus certain skills are often over-represented and others under-represented. This might require you to add, replace, or remove team members, based on a well-defined rationale for the most effective configuration for the team. If you do this, you should meet with the remaining members and explain your decision. If you lack the available resources for changing the membership of the team, you must challenge yourself and the team to determine how to provide what is missing and to manage any excess.

Membership. Once the team has established the principles for determining what sorts of member skills and backgrounds it needs, the team—and each individual—must agree on which specific persons are included in the team. Existing team members should be asked to commit to the goals and operating principles of the team, and given the right to make a dignified exit from the team in case their membership is found to be inappropriate. As the manager, you must be prepared to discuss this issue with team members, either publicly or privately.

Commitment and loyalties. These factors are especially significant for multidisciplinary teams, or for any teams whose members have other organizational "home bases" besides the team itself. Examples of these include product delivery teams consisting of personnel from R&D, manufacturing, and engineering departments; others include consulting groups whose members also belong to the faculty of a university. In any case, unless each member belongs exclusively and full time to the team, the team must challenge each member—repeatedly—to determine her or his priorities and the extent to which the member will support the team's needs when they conflict with those of her or his home base group or organization. Because this may be a delicate subject, you are responsible for demonstrating that it can be discussed legitimately by the team, energetically but without assigning blame, so that the issue can be made clear.

Roles and responsibilities. Over the team's existence, different roles must be enacted by the members, with responsibilities shifting from one person to another. Making this explicit is helpful. Even relatively small matters—such as deciding who will arrange for the meetings, take the notes, report on actions agreed upon, or order coffee—should be made clear, in addition to more substantive issues, such as assigning responsibility for contacting particular suppliers, determining the amount of money someone has the authority to commit, and deciding who must obtain certain important resources.

One extremely useful technique for doing this is **role clarification** (see Beckhard, 1977). This requires a half-day meeting, followed by other meetings to deal with all the issues raised. In essence, you ask the group to list all the important tasks to be done, placing these items in a column on a sheet of newsprint or other large-format display. Put each member's name across the top of the sheet, and form a grid of spaces in which each person's name intersects with each of the things that must be done. The team should then use the following codes to indicate the kind of role or responsibility each person has for each item (the discussion may reveal that some tasks should be subdivided into different jobs, especially if different individuals are responsible for executing smaller elements of them).

- **R = responsible.** This person is accountable for seeing that the item is completed. Assign only one "R" for each task.

- **S = support.** This person is committed to being a resource to the person assigned the "R" for the item, and is expected by management to help accomplish the task.

- **C = consultation.** This person **must** be consulted for "input," advice, and expert opinions, which must be considered in planning and executing the task. A "C" person does not have final approval rights, however. Several "C's" may be assigned for each task.

- **A = approval.** This person reviews the plans and final results for the task, and must either approve them or send them back for specified changes. More than one "A" may be assigned for each task, but it is important that not too many be assigned.

- **I = information.** This person must be kept informed by the person assigned the "R" as to the progress, milestones achieved, and completion of the task, but does not have the formal role of approving or rejecting the work. Several "I's" may be assigned for each task.

Whether or not you use the formal process with your team, you should constantly prompt the team to articulate and agree on its members' roles and responsibilities, and to "update" these agreements as the team's work progresses from the early phases to the completion of major tasks.

Relationships. The issue of relationships is a subtle, personal aspect of a team's life, but it nonetheless remains part of the manager's concerns. Are team members aware of or responding to one another's needs? Does friction or tension exist? Are you, the manager, failing to relate with certain members—or even the whole team—as they would like? This is an important, legitimate topic of discussion. Take time in your conversations with individual team members to ask them if you are meeting their needs. Listen and ask questions, without contradicting or arguing with someone if that person tells you something you dislike or says you could be doing something better. Demonstrate by your behavior that you have heard these concerns. If you cannot make suggested changes, explain why. Refer to these discussions in team meetings. In sum, let your own actions indicate that you consider relationships important, that you are willing to discuss them openly, and that you will try to respond to others' needs. Challenge the other team members to do the same.

Angle 3: The tools

The third corner of the triangle is the team's tools. This category can be expanded infinitely, and encompasses all the procedures, agreements, mechanisms, and other building blocks enabling a team to do its job. For the sake of simplicity, this chapter addresses five major factors. These are not usually thought of as tools, but they are indeed useful "handles" you use to gain "leverage" to improve your team. Your managerial responsibility is to ensure that all of the following are working well for the team by enhancing rather than impeding effectiveness:

- group structure,
- operating principles,
- communication mechanisms,
- environment,
- rewards.

Group structure. If the task is complex and has multiple aspects, many persons—organized functionally—will probably be needed to address portions of the total task. Perhaps a central group must steer and determine overall guidelines. The team may need to be stratified to ensure that different layers of management work at the correct levels, so that no one makes decisions that should be others' responsibility. Even if the task is simple or the team is small, assigning specific tasks to individuals and small groups is helpful. As the manager, you must continually ask yourself—and the team—if the structure is correct for getting a particular part of the job done. If not, the team may have good suggestions for restructuring, although you ultimately have the responsibility for ensuring that the team and its subgroups are set up with the right persons working on the right pieces of the puzzle. Be flexible and creative in reworking the team's structure to fit emerging needs.

Operating principles. Having guidelines for making decisions in a crisis, or for keeping things running smoothly and effectively from day to day, can make all the difference between good and bad performance. For example, a factory production team may develop operating principles such as "Safety takes precedence over everything else," "When starting the machine, always follow procedures X, Y, and Z," and "It is never acceptable to skip a team meeting." A team of negotiators working on a labor contract might have the following operating principles: "Never contradict one another during a meeting," "Begin each meeting with a summary of the previous meeting's agreements," and "Never speak with reporters before the team agrees on what we will say to them."

As the manager, you should explore the topic of operating principles during the team's meetings, and continually develop, publish, and review those that are established. You may decide that some specific principles are non-negotiable, and others may be determined by the team. In any case, you must support and live by your team's operating principles, and insist that the team use them.

Communication mechanisms. You should help the team decide how members want to communicate among themselves and with others outside the team. Meetings are one means of communication. How frequently should meetings be held? Are they mainly for sharing information or for making decisions? Who should attend? What should happen if they do not? How should team members stay in touch if they are working at different locations? What kinds of records should be kept of communications? What sorts of reports and summaries are needed? Often these decisions are left to chance, and a team waits until dissatisfaction or a crisis forces it to improve its communication procedures and mechanisms. You can help the team by pushing it to examine its needs and assumptions **before** a crisis occurs, and to discuss which communication mechanisms are working well and which are not.

The environment. Sometimes a manager does not feel he or she has much control over the environment in which a team works, but one can influence the team's external surroundings and internal "culture" in significant ways. This depends on what the team needs. Perhaps you must relocate the team to a place more conducive to the kind of work to be done, or adapt the space, furniture, or equipment of its current location. You might increase or decrease the team's exposure to management, as appropriate. Maybe you need only do something as simple as helping the team create its own ways of celebrating milestones. Be aware, though, that the environment—both physical and social—makes a difference. The team leader should look for ways to improve that environment so as to increase the team's motivation and effectiveness.

Rewards. You may consider it strange to describe rewards as a tool, but a whole array of rewards are available for motivating a team and encouraging its progress. As its manager, you have direct control over, or at least influence on, the formal rewards (both financial and career) the system provides for the team members. Therefore, the standards should be clear for what is considered excellent, good, normal, acceptable, and inferior performance, and formal rewards should be given in ways that team members find appropriate and fair.

Financial and career rewards, however, are only some of the available means of encouraging a team. Small, frequent expressions of approval may have even more influence. Dropping by to tell someone how much you appreciated an extra effort, noting your gratitude in the margin of a good report produced under difficult conditions, giving individuals small mementos to commemorate the team's milestones, inviting the team to an event outside the organization, allowing members who have worked extra hours unpaid to take "off-the-record" time off to be with their loved ones—all of these small acts of appreciation add up to a significant motivational impact, which can dramatically build a sense of pride and team spirit. As you set the tone with such gestures of personal and professional recognition, you will likely find that the rest of the team also develops the habit of expressing appreciation and support for one another—and, not incidentally, for you.

Summary

Building a team is an ongoing process, one in which the manager plays a pivotal role. You must begin with a vision of what you want the team to be. You must also help the team move steadily through its stages of development, ensuring that the members relate well to one another and to you. Finally, you must work with the group to establish a solid foundation on the "basic triangle" of task, team, and tools. In creating an energetic, smoothly functioning, mutually supportive, and productive team, you are the deciding factor. If you do a good job of it, you will have the privilege of seeing a true team develop, and of knowing that this could not have happened without you.

REFERENCES

Beckhard, R. (1977). *Organizational transitions*. Reading, MA: Addison-Wesley.

Porter, L., & Mohr, B. (Eds). (1982). *Reading book for human relations training*. Arlington, VA: NTL Institute.

How To Stay in Charge—Even with a Consultant

Richard E. Byrd

Some years ago, Haim Ginott wrote a book entitled *Between Parent and Child*. He followed this with sequels, including *Between Teacher and Student* and *Between Parent and Teenager*. Many readers felt Ginott's techniques helped them. A psychiatrist friend of mine, however, commented that he thought these techniques "got between the parent and child." That statement impressed me, for I have seen third-party helpers—such as counselors, school psychologists, therapists, clergy, teachers, and attorneys—through their techniques unintentionally become more a part of a problem than a solution.

In team building activities, the same potential difficulty exists. The organization development (OD) consultant can, in good faith, make a greater contribution to the problem than to the solution by coming between a boss and a team.

Does this mean that managers should avoid using consultants in team building? No, but it does mean managers must remain in charge of the team development process and not turn it over to a consultant who may become the acting boss.

Just as a social worker has a place in helping with the parenting process, or a member of the clergy in helping the laity establish values, the OD consultant may appropriately work with managers and their units. But this consultant's place is **not between** the boss and the team. One frustrated manager resented my coming between him and his team. One evening, after we had completed what I considered a particularly good team building session, he told me, "I want you to help me be a better team leader, not make me look like an ass by taking charge of my team yourself!" That comment puts the matter "on the table" for all OD consultants.

How consultants take over

1. Methodology. The type of learning design can lead to consultants' coming between bosses and their teams. For example, if they use the McBer, Blake Grid, or Kepner-Tregoe methods, or "stand-up" methods such as the EST-type or Weir-type personal growth approaches, then they probably view all groups as "classes" for which they are responsible, although—if asked—they might deny this allegation. Such consultants may use experiential techniques such as role play, role reversal, and power exercises, as though they were working in a typical training setting. They see their role as that of trainer and program deliverer. Managers, in effect, are made temporary members of their own teams as the consultants direct the events.

2. Needs. Consultants can also come between bosses and teams by exercising their interpersonal needs for power and achievement (Atkinson, 1958; McClelland, 1961; Schutz, 1958). I have observed consultants who, although they ask all the "right" questions and make all the "right" moves, are unaware of their own unconscious and unhealthy reactions to their clients' ambivalence, naivete, and recalcitrant behavior, or to perceived weakness and incompetence on the part of the managers. These consultants thus cope with developmental needs by manipulating the managers into acting in ways the consultants feel **they** would act under the same circumstances, or by actually moving in and taking over the teams.

Consultants with excessive power needs—or, in Schutz's terminology, the "need to control"—can subtly and sometimes overtly move between bosses and teams with the clear intention of improving the situation. When this happens, the boss is temporarily replaced and the consultant becomes the surrogate boss. The manager therefore gets little practice in being a new kind of boss, and little personal growth occurs on the job for either the boss or the team.

Change takes place in an organization primarily when it results from the manager's motivation for personal change and/or change in the ways work is accomplished. Bosses must understand what they want and then take personal risks to achieve their goals. When consultants come between bosses and their teams, they destroy bosses' motivation to take risks, even though during the "helping" session a consultant may appear to enhance the motivation of the team itself. If teams see that their bosses are resisting change back on the job, the teams will lose their motivation, with the result that (to quote St. Matthew) "the last state of that man is worse than the first." Thus, the alleged goals of the consultant are frustrated.

3. Leadership. Consultants may also come between bosses and their teams by adopting a messianic posture, thus assuming the role of advocate and speaker for the team. Managers do not need this; certainly they do not need to pay an outsider for this dubious "benefit." Clients must ensure that they do not hire consultants with histories of assuming this posture with other clients.

Experienced consultants know they are only temporarily part of the team. Although modeling is an important tool, advocating against the boss—only to prove this can be done or to "change the boss"—can only increase the risks to everyone's careers.

To managers reading this chapter, I hasten to note that hiring a third-party OD consultant is important for developing an effective management team. The following discussion focuses on the problems associated with using OD consultants, but I emphasize that the potential benefits far outweigh the risks. A mature consultant can help your team develop

- more team leadership skills for you,
- greater commitment to the task, to one another, and to you,
- more effective communication,
- increased trust and understanding among team members,
- strategies for maximizing the collective effort,
- greater clarity and acceptance of one another's contributions, and
- new and more effective working ground rules and processes.

OD consultants can bring fresh perspectives and special observational and intervention skills to a team that can halt ineffective behavior and dysfunctional team patterns, thus freeing the team to fulfill its potential to the extent of its resources. Larry Porter once described the client's desired outcome as "the relief and 'freeing up' I experience when my consultant, sensing my discomfort, responds to it in ways that push me forward but still let me be me."

Because a major requirement of management is the ability to anticipate and prepare for what is to come, let us examine some specific experiences bosses may have as a result of a consultant's well-intentioned attempts to "help." This set of examples is not all inclusive—we each could add to it from our own experiences—but is a good beginning.

Disorientation

By setting up team building interventions or other similar, unfamiliar situations for bosses, consultants may disorient them. Many bosses feel intimidated by OD terminology and special settings. Often they cannot identify what they feel, or will not admit to it if they can. These feelings may lead bosses to feel unfairly exposed in front of their teams. Consultants may make the intervention move faster than they anticipated. They may also not sufficiently include the managers in planning the activity so as to ensure that their involvement will not be passive or dependent.

The ambiguity created "to encourage greater candor" may cause managers to act bizarrely as they perceive they must struggle to survive as bosses. When the manager realizes that the consultant has established and knows the rules—and that the manager does not—the manager will likely withdraw or become extremely aggressive. Bosses may then seek to form coalitions with team members to act against consultants, to abdicate, or even to leave entirely. Faced with these circumstances, bosses may also simply remain calm and try to survive the perceived threat.

Impotence/omnipotence

Consultants usually create circumstances—such as workshops on management or human relations, off-site team building interventions, and interview settings—in which they can best demonstrate their skills. This results in giving consultants' skills in accurately empathizing, confronting issues, sharing insights on the group process, making presentations, and the like the ideal backdrop. Believing that they themselves lack these skills, managers may have hired consultants only to be put in strange settings that may exaggerate their weaknesses further. These bosses, along with their teams, may become overly dependent and ascribe omnipotence—even omniscience—to the consultant, resulting in impotence in the manager and sometimes in team members.

When extreme dependence develops, client bosses may perceive that their problems are worse than they really are and that they are powerless to change things. As one might expect, they will likely come to consider the consultants the only persons they can turn to. If, however, managers resist any feelings of dependence, they may rebel and fail to develop the initial, appropriate level of dependency necessary for allowing consultants to suggest alternative approaches.

Subversion

Sometimes consultants are hired when managers acknowledge that their styles are not sufficiently participative and want to discover new approaches.

If a consultant in such a case discovers and overreacts to the boss's authoritarian, apparently arbitrary actions, this consultant may begin to identify with the "downtrodden" subordinates rather than the manager, much like a marriage counselor who identifies with the "aggrieved" party. The consultant may unconsciously lead a "revolution" under the guise of "facilitating communication." Alternatively, the consultant may find that the boss and team have decided that the situation is acceptable, and that the consultant is the one with the problem.

When consultants get caught up in subversion, bosses may first simply be confused by this behavior, especially if the consultants offer slick rationalizations as to why managers should not feel they are getting "beaten up," but instead recognize that they are "growing." Managers who are seduced by these rationalizations are being led toward increased guilt and self-blame.

Consultant transference

In my experience, many OD consultants seek the life of a "lone ranger" because they do not like being told what to do. They become independent consultants so that they can be independent. Often this need for autonomy and independence is rooted in anger and defiance.

This means that some consultants have problems with authority. They have disliked the bosses they have had, perhaps beginning with those they confronted in their cradles. So they choose to boss instead. The client managers of such consultants may find that these consultants overreact negatively to behavior these managers consider normal managerial practice. The consultants' negative reactions to the client may stem from their earlier unhappy experiences, now transferred to their present clients because of perceived similarities between these clients and the consultants' earlier nemeses.

All consultants—and clients—conduct some transference that they may or may not recognize. Occasionally transference results in the consultant's feeling excessively threatened or overly intimidated by the client. When the consultant behaves more passively or compliantly, the boss and/or team may become disenchanted with this consultant, implicitly realizing that this person is ineffective.

Countertransference

Countertransference is a complicated issue. During countertransference, one reacts toward another person inappropriately in light of the current situation, basing one's actions on one's previous experiences with persons like this other individual. The second person responds to the first person's inappropriate reactions with reactions that are also inappropriate. That is, the pathologies of both persons compound each other.

For example, a client who belongs to a minority group may react angrily toward what he considers racist behavior by the consultant. The consultant, however, is convinced that he is not a racist. Because of previous experiences with hostile persons from minority groups, the consultant responds defensively and thus compounds the problem. This only reinforces the client's original transference issue: that persons who act like the consultant are racist.

Too many consultants get into countertransference without realizing it until too late. Potential consultant transference can be represented by a statement such as "I hate bosses"; potential consultant countertransference can be represented by a statement such as "I hate bosses who act as if they hate me." As with the phenomenon of transference discussed above, high degrees of countertransference distort the consultant-client relationship and provide distorted examples for team members.

Calvinism

Sometimes those helping clients develop an unconscious set of behaviors labeled "consultant Calvinism," which can be described as "teacher knows best."

In this context, Calvinism refers to the "ought to" that comes to consultants' minds when they consider their clients' management skills inadequate. They measure this inadequacy by comparing what they believe they could do to that done by the "nincompoop." In this situation, consultants no longer feel responsible primarily for providing clients with "input," but instead with turning clients into clones who will produce their own desired "output."

This odious comparison results in consultants' developing an underlying lack of respect for bosses. If bosses do not learn fast enough, do not appear sufficiently motivated, disagree with the consultants, hear a "different drummer," or are less task or achievement oriented, the consultants become increasingly strident in demanding change.

Under these circumstances, consultants will state that unbelievably bad consequences can issue from clients' failing to do what consultants propose to be correct. Sometimes consultants will "wash their hands" of clients—that is, take no responsibility for the interventions' outcomes. Sometimes the consultants seek to hide their feelings, but manage to let others in the organization know their opinions—even to the point of acting as catalysts for movements opposing the bosses. Such attitudes may divide a team from its boss and cause it to perceive the boss as a "bad person." The consultant's behavior confirms the team's worst fears, reinforces its members' own pathologies about bosses, and generally destroys productive relationships. In the most severe cases, consultants may even manipulate situations so as to ingratiate themselves with their clients' superiors and replace the bosses.

To understand consultant Calvinism, listen to consultants when they are not with their clients. If they gossip or laugh about their clients behind their backs, this indicates disrespect and passive-aggressive dynamics that may harm a team. These behaviors reflect an attitude of superiority that the consultant communicates to the client in both direct and subliminal ways, ironically in the name of wanting to be of help.

Looking for a fix

Some OD consultants get hooked on exciting personal and human experiences. They approach team building looking for a "fix." The more conflict they can engender, the more hidden agenda they can surface, the greater the "high" they can get. In the 1960s, some "just plain folks" became human relations laboratory "tramps," traveling from laboratory to laboratory to maintain their state of intoxication. OD consultants sometimes unconsciously look for a personal fix at the expense of bosses and their teams.

To be sure, if consultants deal only with surface interactions, the previously noted benefits of team building will not be realized. But delicate political and career issues must be handled carefully and with great aplomb. Furthermore, as Ken Benne—the inventor of the phrase "hidden agenda"—has noted, "Some agenda deserve to remain hidden." An OD consultant's need for "real dialogue," tears, hugging, or physical "acting out" of any sort may hinder team development.

Keeping the boss in charge

Some of the unconscious bad habits and mild pathologies of consultants may not be subject to change. An old story speaks of mutual happiness developing between a sadist and a masochist; perhaps consultants find bosses who actually like the consultants' negative qualities.

Assuming, however, that relationships should be governed by a minimum of mental health problems, the rest of this chapter is dedicated to helping both managers and OD consultants prevent the development of the kinds of problems described above. The following sections contain what I suggest are reasonable expectations for client bosses to have for the consultants they hire, along with descriptions of consultant behaviors I have personally found helpful in keeping myself from coming between bosses and their teams.

1. Client bosses: Expect your consultants to accept you as you are, warts and all. You should expect patience and an assumption of good will from your OD consultant.

Consultants: Move at your clients' level of understanding and ability to cope. If a client is too slow or stupid for you to tolerate, quit. Do not let anger and frustration build, whether it is your own or the team's. Assume that bosses are doing what they consider their best. Use your impatience to stimulate a self-examination of your own motivation.

2. Client bosses: Expect your consultants to be your personal advocates. You are taking some personal and career risks with the intervention, so demand that the consultant recognize those risks. If the chemistry is not right between you two, the consultant may abandon you in a crunch. Choose carefully and expect the consultant to work toward your goals. Do not, however, demand that the consultant merely do your bidding; that would be a waste of the investment.

Consultants: Make sure you treat the bosses as your clients. If you treat "the group" as your client, you will be considered naive, for "everyone knows" that bosses must take the major risks. The team will not believe you if you say that you are no more the boss's consultant than theirs. Besides, by being a consultant to the boss, you keep from getting between the boss and the team. This means the team knows not to look to you to "save" it, but instead will look to the boss who has sought your help in getting the desired results.

3. Client bosses: Expect to be in charge during the team building session. Personally plan every step with the consultant; do not turn this task over to anyone else, not even your assistant. When a meeting is held, make sure you call it to order. Introduce the process and, based upon your planning with the consultant, handle all the administration, timing, decisions on moving on, and proposed action steps. Although you may be a powerful member of the group, do not generally seek to control the actual overall direction of the conversation more than any other member of the group. But remember that if you turn the meeting over to the consultant, your team will not consider it a "real" meeting.

Consultants: Keep bosses in charge of any interventions. The client may keep trying to get you to assume a responsibility that belongs to the client. Do not give in to the boss's demands unless you have identified what is happening and the potential consequences of your doing what is asked. That is, deliberately choose to do it. The goals of the intervention should be stated in the words of the client boss. If you provide information for a memorandum, make sure the client changes this into the client's own language and signs her or his name to the memo. Be adamant about this. Every time you allow your name to be used in anything but an adjunct capacity, you come between the boss and the team.

Only in a T Group of strangers or a therapy group should members be of equal status and the consultants or therapists hold leadership roles. In the structured world of management, only when we are playing games do bosses fail to act as bosses. If the boss chairs group meetings on all important occasions, then the boss had better act as chair during the team building intervention, or else none of the team members will believe the event is anything but a charade. This allows you, the consultant, to have more time to process group action, and the boss to have the responsibility for the group's productivity. The boss will also be in a position to cut you off if he or she thinks you are out of line or dominating the event. The boss must be the boss. Your job is to help the boss do this job better, not to take the boss's place.

For some team building activities, you have the words, techniques, and skills clients need. For others, you must let the clients work out the problems themselves. Knowing when and how to use third-party intervention is important to helping clients distinguish between legitimate and illegitimate dependency.

4. Client bosses: Expect to spend time working one on one with your consultants. Discuss your philosophy of management, what you want from the team building, and your previous experience with OD consultants or other technical advisors. Interview potential consultants as you would candidates for any valuable position. Learn what makes them tick; invite them to staff meetings; talk with them afterward to learn what they observed that you missed. Get comfortable with them.

Consultants: Do not prescribe team building too quickly. Take your time. Meet the client boss, possibly some team members. Get a good idea of what they are about, whether you can respect them and accept their goals as your own, and whether the chemistry is right. Make sure they do not immediately trigger the previously discussed pathologies in you. Make sure they feel comfortable with you—and you with them—before moving ahead.

5. Client bosses: Expect consultants to control the boundaries for risk, both for themselves and for team members. Ask to be kept informed constantly of what the consultant is doing, without asking for the names of any "culprits" or demanding to edit any data you consider threatening. Let the consultant explain the rationale for doing something, and expect some risk taking by everyone—it is necessary for growth.

Consultants: Seek to reduce unnecessary risks for client bosses rather than increase them (Byrd, 1974, pp. 113-159). Clients do not need you to tell them how to get into trouble. For example, needless fights with consistently petulant team members should not be encouraged. I consider OD a way for bosses to increase the flow of information they need to manage. To get this information flowing from and to their teams, they may need to take some personal risks. You must help the boss by supporting risk taking and enabling the boss to see the consequences of whatever he or she does. Work with your client in solving problems.

Show the boss any reports you have prepared before you share these reports with the entire team during a diagnostic activity. This is so you can help the boss understand the reports and be prepared for the team's reaction. Looking at data in advance does not mean giving the boss time to edit them, although occasionally I have edited reports following a discussion with the boss in which potentially destructive consequences were noted.

6. Client bosses: Expect consultants to work out transference and/or countertransference issues. You should not have to worry about such psychological factors unless those factors become counterproductive for the team. If you think your consultant is angrier with you or more devoted to you than your instincts consider reasonable, you may have a problem. Check with a trusted member of your team to ensure that you are not overreacting; if you find you are not, confront the consultant. If the consultant's response to this is thoughtful, you probably should continue working with that person. If the consultant reacts defensively, you should consider getting another consultant. Trust your feelings.

Consultants: If you become aware of transference and/or countertransference issues, work them out directly with your clients. I generally prefer to do this privately, putting the burden on myself to assure clients that they are normal, that transference is a natural phenomenon that may underlie all human bonding. You may need, however, to talk with clients about their behavior when they appear to be treating you as a son or daughter, in either the best or worst sense. Teams will not accept this, so bosses need to see it, even if they cannot change the behavior. If you are acting like a son or daughter to the boss, you may be compounding the problem. This kind of situation obviously is complex, and may sometimes require another consultant to work out the dysfunctional aspects. If correcting the problem seems impossible, consider resigning for the client's sake.

7. Client bosses: Expect to be confronted by your consultants. The power structure allows you, the boss, to prevent insubordination, ensure compliance with corporate goals, receive deferential treatment in accordance with your role, and generally control the situation. You have created some of this structure, but most of it has developed because of each team member's personal history and the culture of your organization.

Although a stable pecking order has clear benefits, it also has clear liabilities, such as less-than-candid appraisals by team members of propositions you support, fear of reprisal, fear that the messenger carrying bad news will be shot, limits on creativity, assumptions of what you do and do not want, and the like. The consultants will use skill (we hope) to shatter the assumptions that may inhibit team effectiveness. The consultant will also confront team members, who also help create overly stable group dynamics impeding development.

Consultants: In the team setting, act as models for confronting bosses. People learn by identifying with such behavior. You should also be free to protect the team members from excessive openness, which they may not realize can destroy the work group. The more mature and skillful the group, the less likely is the consultant to have to do the monitoring.[1] If, however, no one on the team will confront the boss, you must do so. If you have been straightforward with your client, the client will trust that you are doing this with the client's interests in mind, not your own.

Summary and conclusion

In this chapter, I try to describe how OD consultants may fall into the trap of coming between bosses and their teams. I suggest that consultants sometimes use inappropriate learning methods, have excessive personal needs, provide the wrong kind of leadership, or become caught up in transference and/or countertransference phenomena. The negative result of this is that the goal of the consulting—instituting change—is not accomplished by the "turned-off" manager.

I also suggest some appropriate ways to ensure—as much as possible—that consultants work on clients' problems rather than their own. The consultant's goal should be to make managers smarter rather than stupider in working with their teams, first by believing their expressed intention to change even when the behavior seems dissonant, and second by accepting that the managers are the captains of their own fates. The bosses must assess risks and, with their teams, make all the final decisions but one.

The one decision left to the consultant is that of whether or not to work with a given client. If consultants finding themselves coming between bosses and their teams, and thus acting destructively, they should exercise their option—and get out of the way.

NOTE

1. Overall, I trust people to sense their own limits. But I remember the day my two-year-old daughter walked off the edge of a swimming pool into eight feet of water. She did not recognize the danger.

REFERENCES

Atkinson, J. W. (Ed.). (1958). *Motives in fantasy, action and society.* Princeton, NJ: Van Nostrand.

Byrd, R. E. (1974). *A guide to personal risk taking.* New York: AMACOM.

McClelland, D. C. (1961). *The achieving society.* Princeton, NJ: Van Nostrand.

Schutz, W. C. (1958, July-August). Interpersonal underworld. *Harvard Business Review, 34*(4), 123-135.

The Newcomer and the Ongoing Work Group

Herman Gadon

The literature on teams and task groups largely ignores the issues raised by the entry of newcomers into established, ongoing work groups. This chapter identifies those issues and provides a model to help newcomers, group members, and managers cope with these issues more effectively.

Imagine you have just been hired, promoted, transferred, or demoted, and have joined a work group that has existed for a long time. Although the circumstances for joining seem radically different, each one will force you to confront similar issues during the next few months. No matter how likeable and competent you are, or well known by the persons whose group you will join, you will in some way be a disrupting influence.

Case example

Eddy Martin left his job as manager of a branch bank in a medium-sized Midwestern city as a much-loved figure. One of the first persons hired by the branch, he had contributed substantially to its rapid growth, and was frequently called on by other branch managers to help them solve their problems. Eddy was also much appreciated by his subordinates, whom he encouraged to assume responsibilities they had previously thought beyond their abilities. Relationships among bank employees were close; they always seemed to be having a party to celebrate a birthday, new baby, marriage, or even the winning of a new account. A family atmosphere existed, with little turnover and all the employees' feeling as if they had grown up together. Recognized for its high performance, the branch was known as a good place to work.

Buoyed by his success at the bank, Eddy went with high hopes to his new job as director of business development for a small insurance company in Portland, Oregon. He felt wanted by the company he was joining, whose president, Hal Stephenson, had been courting him for some time. Hal believed the company had unrealized potential and wanted Eddy to help it grow more rapidly. Knowing that Hal expected to step aside in a few years, Eddy also thought he saw an opportunity to take Hal's place.

Because he had been brought in by the company president, Eddy was treated with solicitude by his new colleagues, who went out of their way to introduce him to the "ins and outs" of insurance. At first, things seemed to go well. Eddy did not initiate much, but instead watched, read, allowed himself to be taught by others, learned fast, and began to get a good grasp of the business.

After two months Eddy thought he saw how he could make a significant impact on the company's prospects for growth. Furthermore, convinced that he had been hired with the hope that he might be Hal's successor, he felt the time had come to demonstrate that he had the vision and capability to lead the business to a bright future. He felt ready to assert himself, and he did. He challenged the way the firm had been doing business, urging a major investment in a new line of business and radical changes in the approaches to marketing. He knew his recommendations would be unsettling to Robert, a long-time employee who was primarily responsible for how the company then did business. But Eddy's confidence in his own proposals was so great he was sure they would soon be appreciated.

The results were disquieting. Hal became less available to Eddy and began to relay messages to him through Robert. Others' attitudes also changed. They became more brusque with Eddy and sometimes impatient with his questions. Several times in staff meetings he was surprised to find himself defending a minority position, supported only by the office manager. He was particularly disappointed in how his relationship with Rita, the marketing manager, was developing: They had liked each other at the beginning, yet their relationship had since cooled. Tensions mounted steadily thereafter, and by his sixth month with the company Eddy had become isolated.

Frustrated and unhappy, Eddy was pleased when he received a generous offer to return to banking, this time as the manager of a sizeable branch in Austin, Texas, with excellent career prospects. Given his recent experience in Portland, Eddy was tempted to leave the insurance company, but reluctant to write off the experience he had had in establishing himself in the insurance industry, and with a firm that was apparently ready to "take off." Confrontations with Hal, Robert, and Rita finally cleared the air. Eddy shared with them his hopes of succeeding Hal. They revealed that they resented his efforts to replace Robert as heir apparent to the company president. Robert was respected and had developed with the business, and the group would not allow him to be usurped by a pretentious newcomer, no matter how bright and imaginative. Eddy's goal was considered inappropriate, and therefore efforts had been made to put him in his place. Rita's change in attitude stemmed from this: She had liked Eddy at first and had looked forward to having his help in marketing, but when she realized what his ambition was, she was unwilling to encourage him and so, along with the others, had rejected his recommendations in order to cut him down to size.

Realizing that he was going to be relegated to a lower position in the management team was painful for Eddy. Disappointment and wounded pride almost pushed him into leaving the firm. He had difficulty accepting the situation and giving up—at least at that time—his dream of assuming the presidency soon. He did, however, still see opportunities to grow with the firm, which he found rewarding enough for the present. Consequently, he made a commitment to stay, based on new and more realistic perceptions of the place he would be allowed to occupy in the organization.

Afterward communications with others improved and staff spirit and morale rose following the successful resolution of the conflict. Eddy's ideas began to be evaluated for their true merits, and his performance exceeded anyone's expectations. To the casual observer, the work group appeared to function much as it had before Eddy's arrival; many of the folkways were preserved as the team survived Eddy's entry and absorbed him into its structure. This sense of continuity only masked the differences, though, for careful scrutiny would have revealed changes in roles, relationships, and decision-making processes. After the confrontation, members of the management team talked with one another more openly, and issues previously avoided were now faced as they arose. Cooperation became easier and was expected. The hierarchy had affirmed some positions and shifted others to make room for Eddy. Thus, his coming actually precipitated the death and rebirth of the group. It looked a lot as it had before, yet was different. With the addition of a newcomer, it had actually become a new group.

Each work group has a life and personality of its own. Like individuals, work groups develop over time and have clearly distinguishable personalities that tend to persist and resist change. Some groups are happy, some tense, some barely productive; others are effective and congenial. In whatever ways they have evolved, with whatever qualities, and whether or not their members like them, work groups that have been in existence for some time have characteristics that are known to their members, and the part each member plays is known to all the others. Newcomers threaten the patterns to which members of an established team have become accustomed, therefore creating discomfort and unsettling the environment until the new persons are accepted and new routines affirmed. Although a work group will pressure a newcomer to conform to its expectations—to enable it to go on as it had before—the entry of every newcomer induces a new life cycle for the group.

This life cycle represents a process of maturation. Not only do **new** groups go through this process in a predictable succession of steps, but ongoing groups absorbing new members also go through it. The failure of established groups to recognize that they too, like newly formed groups, must undergo again the development process whenever they receive newcomers often causes them untold and unnecessary distress.

If Eddy, Hal, and his colleagues had been able to anticipate the pressures Eddy's entry into the group precipitated, they might have been able to help him become integrated faster, more constructively, and with less difficulty. In Eddy's case, the organization was fortunate because, although everyone muddled around for a while, the outcome was ultimately satisfactory. Many cases do not work out so well. Sometimes newcomers give up trying and—in frustration—leave the organization, veterans whom the company values quit with feelings of being betrayed, or work groups reorganize themselves with uncertain results. Understanding the stages groups go through after they are first formed, or after a new person enters an established group, will help managers, newcomers, and group members anticipate the feelings and events they are likely to face during the development process. Armed with this knowledge, they will be in a position to choose appropriate behaviors. The next section helps readers understand these processes.

The development of work groups

Many different kinds of work groups exist. Some are temporary, created to achieve a given purpose. The existence of these groups continues until an assigned task is completed. Such groups include project teams, task forces, and committees. Other work groups are permanent parts of their organizations, woven into the fabric of their basic structures. Permanent groups have no anticipated end and continue until the organization changes. These groups include departments, sections, production units, and management teams such as the one Eddy was in.

If one maintains membership simultaneously in two groups, that person is said to be in a matrix, an organizational form popularized by the aerospace industry. In that industry, professionals in engineering departments emphasizing particular functions—such as mechanical, electrical, electronic, hydraulic, and propulsion engineers—are often "loaned" to a project team that has been created to design an aircraft, such as the Boeing 747. These persons thus have two bases of membership, the permanent one of one's "home" department and the temporary one of the project group. A person at work who is assigned to a committee or task force is similarly in a matrix. Matrix structures complicate the lives of the persons who are in them because they inspire divided loyalties.

Nevertheless, every new work group, and every existing group getting a new member—whether or not it is in a matrix, whether it is temporary or permanent—goes through a process of development that corresponds to maturation. But just as an individual can get stuck at some stage in her or his life, a group too can sometimes fail to make healthy progress. When groups fail to mature, they—like individuals who remain immature—do not realize their potential and are less effective than they could be.

Fortunately, the predictability of the process of development, if understood, can help established groups improve their ability to integrate new members.

The stages of group development

As groups develop, they go through the following stages:

- **Stage 1: Connecting**—characterized by orienting, forming, finding support, learning **who is in and who is out;**
- **Stage 2: Competing**—characterized by confronting, controlling, positioning, learning **who is up and who is down;**
- **Stage 3: Collaborating**—characterized by accepting, differentiating, accommodating, learning to **live and let live;**
- **Stage 4: Caring**—characterized by encouraging, developing, supporting, contributing according to ability and interests, learning to **give and take on one's merits.**

Stage 1: Connecting

Persons new to a group must earn membership in it. Even if this individual is known by the other members before joining, he or she still has to "fit in," and no one can be certain ahead of time exactly how—or even if—this will be accomplished. Therefore, some excitement, anxiety, and hesitant behavior always exists when a new person enters an ongoing group.

Hesitancy is a function of unfamiliarity. Not knowing what will take place or how to respond to the uncertainty, newcomers are appropriately cautious at the beginning. Despite their being guarded, however, they each tend to have their own entry style, or way of coping with early discomfort. Some are noisy, taking a lot of space and making themselves visible. Others are inclined to watch and listen, saying little and "laying low" until they can figure out what is happening. An entry style is developed over a lifetime, and is a reflexive, characteristic way of reacting to a new situation. A colleague and I tend to enter new groups differently. One of us is generally assertive, lively, and eager to leap the hurdle of anonymity; the other tends to be more observant and quiet, sizing others up before speaking. Although our entry styles are different, we have the same objectives. We first "feel out" the situation, looking for indications of how other group members react to us, what the group is like, what kind of membership is possible, what effect one can have, and what is required for full acceptance. Bill Irwin, a renowned clown and comic genius who won a MacArthur Foundation prize in 1984 in recognition of his talent, described his way of making first connections:

> One of the lessons I learned was to wait, whether I was moving to a new city or walking into a party. . . . Trying to be assertive too soon was almost always going to work against me. I have the same set of instincts in performing. First, I get the lay of the land. (Gussow, 1985, p. 55)

As in the case of Irwin, a newcomer's reflexive behavior when in unfamiliar territory is a function of previous experiences. By thinking about the way you have dealt with new situations, you can recognize your own pattern. If it has served you well, you will want to stick with it. If you do not like the results of it, you can practice changing your behavior. By becoming aware of it, you have some choices, even though changing a firmly entrenched habit takes considerable effort and patience with yourself. Much time is needed to learn to do something new, and you must be able to tolerate some mistakes.

Fortunately, out of politeness and a general belief that newcomers should be treated courteously, the group usually allows new arrivals a grace period in which to prove themselves worthy of membership, giving them the benefit of the doubt until evidence suggests a harsher judgment. Some, however, are discounted from the beginning. Rather than receiving the benefit of the doubt, they must overcome negative feelings about them; this frequently occurs when a newcomer replaces a member whom the others greatly cared for. The newcomer is labeled as "not good enough" to fill the position of the person who left.

Not only are newcomers sometimes labeled, but they may also be stereotyped, particularly if they belong to a minority group. Stereotypes are not in themselves always bad: We dislike uncertainty and look for cues to tell us how to treat a person and predict how he or she will respond. The fewer signals we get, the more likely we are to rely on stereotypes. That is why I urge you, if you are a newcomer, to let others see you as a person as early as possible. You do not have to be too indiscreet or personal; self-disclosure is not as helpful as expressiveness. React by smiling when a joke is told, telling one in return, offering to help with a problem, joining the group for a drink after work, letting others know how you behave in different circumstances. The opposite of this is wearing a "poker face," which is intended to keep others from knowing what you think or feel: It is great for gambling, but not for making relationships.

If stereotypes persist in the face of evidence to the contrary, then prejudice is present. This can be a stubborn problem, and one whose importance should not be overlooked. Prejudice, however, is harder to sustain in small, face-to-face groups when it is contradicted by first-hand knowledge. The group's acceptance of it will also be affected by the norms, or informal rules, emerging in the group. Groups can evolve with norms that reject prejudice or reinforce it (the discussion of Stage 3 examines the emergence of norms, the turns they can take, and their consequences).

The process of knowing others and becoming known seldom occurs among all group members at the same time. Rather, one quickly recognizes the one or two other group members with whom one initially feels more comfortable, with whom one shares "good vibes." This is hardly surprising: We intuitively scan the group for persons with whom we can connect, and we have difficulty remembering and relating simultaneously to a lot of new people, and so tend to respond gratefully to whoever shows us some sign of approval. Approval causes anxiety to decrease and gives one the courage to reach out to others.

The danger is that clinging too strongly to one attachment may cause a person to exclude others and become isolated. The quick formation of subgroups may either facilitate or inhibit group development. If persons reach out to others because they feel more secure after forming a few relationships, the group will keep on growing. If, however, the subgroups become fixed and persons retreat to them, the group's development will slow or stop. With enough splintering, the group may even get stuck and become unable to perform at all. Recognizing the significance of early support, a few companies assign a "buddy" to each newly hired person to help that person break into a work group, and thus do not rely on chance. The buddy system provides a person's first important relationship, and so by design paves the way for the formation of other relationships. Strangely enough, I do not know of any company that assigns buddies to persons who have been transferred, promoted, or demoted, although these transitions are as demanding as that of being hired. Perhaps companies assume that transferred employees are not new in the same sense as newly hired ones, and therefore fail to recognize that such persons are still newcomers to their work groups and could benefit from support from a "buddy."

In addition to becoming known as a person, a newcomer to an ongoing work group must establish her or his ability to contribute to accomplishing the group's tasks. Therefore, considerable curiosity will exist as to the stranger's competence and skill. If you are a newcomer, use your time at the beginning to ensure that you understand what the group's essential work is and how it relates to the organization's objectives. A sure prescription for a bad start is to make pronouncements on work matters before you really know what is going on or before the group is ready to hear them. Timing is crucial: You will likely be resented if you move too soon, even if your are right; if you are wrong, you will undermine your credibility.

The period of early testing has three elements. One is the need for you, the newcomer, to find out what you can do. The second is for the group to find out what kind of person you are. The third is to establish where you fit in in the group's hierarchy. Every group has a pecking order. Therefore, while you are demonstrating your ability so that you can establish your right to be accepted as a worthwhile contributor to achieving the group's tasks, and to show how people can get along with you, you are also vying for a position in the group. If the place you desire coincides with the place the group has reserved for you, your transition to acceptance will be smooth. If you harbor an ambition the group considers illegitimate, you will have to fight for your place. This is the situation in which Eddy found himself. He did as well as one could expect in seeking information, and was respected for the way he did this. Eddy was briefed by Hal, read everything available on insurance, reviewed company files and reports, and sought data from his colleagues. He also waited two months before asserting himself. But when he rejected the place in the management team's pecking order that had been reserved for him and chose instead to challenge Robert for the Number 2 position behind the president, Eddy was ostracized. Only after he gave up his aspirations did the other members of the team fully accept him and work collaboratively with him.

Testing occurs early in the newcomer's work life because everyone is interested in finding out initially if a reasonable fit exists. Usually, however, this testing is done with caution, uncertainty, and tentativeness. Much is to be learned about newcomers, and curiosity is intense. When a group emerges from the first stage, testing takes a different turn. Often, a pecking order is not readily accepted, and thus jostling for influence occurs. By then a reasonable amount of connecting has taken place; members have taken measure of one another, and the group seems to settle down. When signs of increasing tension become apparent—as was the case with Eddy's group—they clearly signal that the group is sliding into the next stage of its development.

Stage 2: Competing

The second stage of group development is likely to be an emotional one, for a lot is at stake. Once rankings are established, they stay in place for a long time. If issues of control are not settled, they will resurface repeatedly and inevitably be disruptive. Groups that continually experience fights over power do not use their resources well and create much dissatisfaction among their members. If ideas are opposed or supported because of who proposed them—rather than on their own merits—one may be reasonably sure that the group is stuck in Stage 2 and recycling power issues. In groups that work well, issues of role, influence, and leadership do not consume the groups' energies.

When members fight for power, they are poor listeners. If you feel defensive, you will be more interested in looking for holes in your adversary's arguments that you can turn to your advantage rather than in understanding that person's position. Such situations also reinforce subgroups, as persons in a fight look for allies and pressure others to take sides. Although struggles to solve Stage 2 differences are sometimes quite obvious—and increasingly so as feelings grow stronger—they may also be subtle and hard to understand. Knowing that such struggles should be expected will prepare you to look for them and to help resolve them so that they do not keep recurring.

Such closure may not be easy to achieve. Generally, success and a constructive outcome are more likely if the real issues are identified, raised, and discussed openly. When locked in a struggle they believe they can win, however, individuals or factions may perceive that suppressing the truth will help their cause. They will therefore oppose any attempt to force them to disclose their motives, fears, aspirations, or alliances. Openness can only be achieved when individuals feel it will make them better off because it makes the group better off when differences are settled—even if some members are unhappy with the results.

Such was the case with Eddy. Once he acknowledged his difficulties and realized he had to choose between leaving and taking his chances on finding out how much support he had in the group, he faced the issue. The confrontation forced him to accept some unpleasant truths, and he might have quit as a consequence, but he chose instead to swallow his pride and accept the relative rank available to him in the group. Once the hierarchy was settled, the group could function well again.

Stage 2 is a phase of sorting out or putting each member in her or his place. Once done, expectations for the everyday work of the group are known and predictable. This does not mean that roles and influence do not shift according to need and ability as circumstances change: High-performing groups are flexible and adaptable. Routine requires order, and this is settled in groups that mature healthily. This phase also need not be a "stormy" one, full of drama and intense struggle. Testing will always occur, both of interpersonal qualities and competence, but it may be hardly noticeable and the results readily accepted. The casual observer of a group developing well with little outward evidence of strain may even protest that the group has skipped this stage. This is not so, although the absence of a dramatic struggle over influence may make things appear this way. The danger of denying that the group underwent a period of competition and sorting out is that this may mean that differences were not resolved. A sign of such unfinished business is unexpected and inappropriate behavior, such as intense opposition to a point that is not warranted. This suggests that persons are still competing for position, but in a covert manner.

Stage 3: Collaborating

Behavior in groups that have successfully navigated their way through Stage 2 is noticeably more relaxed. If the second phase was characterized by much strain—as was the case for Eddy and his colleagues—when that stage ends members will show relief, and impatience to get on with the group's task. Energy that had been diverted because of personal tensions will be available for accomplishing work. By Stage 3, not only have interpersonal differences been settled, but the newcomer's skills have become better known and this person has learned to use them appropriately. Often productivity will jump as a consequence. Success supports other developments, harmony is valued, group solidarity grows in importance, and norms to promote it are reinforced.

Norms are the unwritten rules each member must observe to stay in good standing in the group. In groups with some history, norms are ordinarily so well established that they are relatively unaffected by the entry of a new member. Indeed, the new member will be pressured by colleagues to observe them until this person either conforms or is rejected for failing to do so. Sometimes, though, the prevailing norms are changed as a result of the process of absorbing a new member. In Eddy's case, the resolution of the crisis over his ranking in the group led to more openness in confronting conflicts as soon as they arose.

For Eddy's team, the evolving norms were constructive, but this is not always the case. Norms do not always develop automatically in ways that contribute to an organization's effectiveness or even to the well-being of individual employees. Indeed, they can occasionally be terribly constraining, impairing the abilities of individuals and organizations to achieve their objectives.

An individual faces difficulty holding a view contrary to the opinions of a majority. When this individual is also a newcomer and thus vulnerable, seeking acceptance and approval, the pressure to cave in and go along with the others is nearly overwhelming. By being aware and vigilant, newcomers can at least consciously decide whether to acquiesce or stand firm, rather than losing their sense of self and sacrificing their capacity to make independent judgments. Similarly, managers and groups should also keep this in mind if they want to preserve the opportunity to take advantage of new possibilities presented by the fresh perceptions of a stranger. We can easily take for granted what has been done for some time, as this is more comfortable and less threatening than change, but if one always takes the easier path one loses the opportunity to learn something new.

Norms take various shapes, some social and some based on task. The lists below present some examples.

Some **social norms** include the following:

- who takes coffee and lunch breaks together—hourly workers with hourly workers only, women with women, and managers with managers;
- the length of coffee breaks—20 minutes, even though the official limit is 10 minutes;
- the dress code—managers wear ties, and women wear skirts or dresses, never slacks;
- rituals—participation is required in parties, horseplay, joking, and celebrating;
- the pecking order—during meetings one must always wait for the person with the highest status to speak first.

Some **task norms** include the following:

- hours—one works until the given task is done rather than by the clock;
- information—one readily shares information with all who can use it;
- expertise—one makes one's expertise available according to need, meaning it is freely loaned;
- productivity—this never exceeds a standard that is set informally; meaning it is freely loaned;
- communication—one communicates only through the chain of command, never bypassing one's supervisor or communicating laterally, and with many written memoranda, including those confirming conversations;

- influence—one has influence according to one's formal rank in the organizational hierarchy;
- decision making—one should consult with those expected to be affected by one's decisions.

As one can tell, some norms are functional and others dysfunctional. Whether they are good or bad, however, they are the "organizational cement" holding a group together. Although they reinforce uniformity, they may also provide enough security for members to express some individuality. For example, if the group continues to mature in a healthy progression, an increasing amount of member differentiation will occur with respect to roles, influence, and personal style. During Stage 3, outsiders may note that the group seems to have grown more parochial, tending to exclude nonmembers and thinking in terms of "we versus they." Having successfully worked their way through Stage 2, such groups feel good about themselves and their ability to work well together and become more self-centered. If the group continues to develop, it will become less self-conscious and, with time, more willing to work comfortably with other groups in the organization. Feeling confident that their own group trusts and supports them seems to allow members to shift roles within the group according to the nature of the task and to work with persons in other groups according to the organization's needs. Such nonthreatening adaptability and flexibility characterizes groups that have matured enough to arrive at Stage 4.

Stage 4: Caring

In the fourth stage, groups have fully absorbed newcomers, who thus are no longer differentiated from the others on the basis of how long they have belonged to their groups. No one thinks in terms of newcomers; what counts most is the merits of each person's contribution. Individuals' talents and deficiencies are acknowledged, accepted, and taken into account in the division of labor and allocation of roles. Leadership is exercised by persons best suited to particular circumstances, and is shifted—if useful—when situations change. Appreciation is freely expressed and disagreement considered natural, related to the task, and subject to rational examination. The group members work well as a team or as individuals, depending on what is needed. Because the group is confident of its collective abilities and each member's ability to represent it well, it almost always has good relations with other parts of the organization. Little defensiveness occurs within the group or in the group's exchanges with outsiders.

Tensions never disappear, however, even when the group operates at its highest level of potential. This is because tension is needed to inspire creativity. When persons or groups must reconcile contradictions, they are most likely to be imaginative and productive. Jim Webb, the brilliant man who was NASA's first director, found that diverse points of view forced groups in NASA to reexamine assumptions, thus providing the bases for new discoveries. He therefore insisted on bringing persons from many disciplines together to solve problems rather than building teams of engineers and scientists with the same backgrounds.

A study made during World War II found that the most effective bomber crews were not those with either the most or the least tension, but those with moderate amounts of tension, which spurred them to cope creatively with unexpected events. One often hears that groups get complacent or self-satisfied, and that this is ultimately harmful to their productivity. Without tension, a group is not stimulated to reexamine how it does things. The arrival of a newcomer often shakes up such groups, introducing new ideas. A prominent company in the service industry that previously selected its presidents from within its own ranks has recently begun searching for an outsider to replace the soon-to-retire chief executive—acting out of the belief that this is the best way for the company to remain innovative in an increasingly competitive environment. Newcomers who slip into a group almost unnoticed may do little to disrupt its comfort, but may also deprive the group of an opportunity to function in new, more imaginative ways.

Because groups gravitate naturally toward bending newcomers to the group's will, one must recognize that potential learning may be lost as a consequence. Such a practice makes groups lose the benefit of seeing themselves through the eyes of a stranger, and this opportunity cannot be recovered after the newcomer is absorbed. Remember how odd, colorful, or bizarre new situations have seem to you: People from the tropics seeing their first snowstorm find it almost indescribable, as does a northerner seeing palm trees for the first time. After you have gotten used to new circumstances, however, you hardly notice what goes on around you. I remember my first days in a well-established company. After attending a few of the regular weekly meetings of departmental managers held by the vice president of operations, I realized I was the only one who ever came on time. Because my time was as valuable as anyone else's, and I was unwilling to challenge the group's norms so soon after joining the firm, I, too, gradually began arriving later and later to meetings. Fortunately, at one of the meetings the vice president asked me for my newcomer's impressions. My observation of the lack of concern for promptness provoked a discussion that revealed that everyone had simply taken this for granted for so long that no one noticed it any longer. This led to other observations that were equally surprising and valuable.

To salvage fresh insights before they become dull from time and therefore lost forever, newcomers should be interviewed after their first month in the work group. This could be done by the new person's immediate supervisor, by someone in the human resources department, or by all the group members when they are all together. The group setting will likely produce a more positive response to the interview, as it helps the newcomer avoid feeling as if he or she is "telling tales out of school." The openness of the process will also signal that disclosure is welcome. Still, such procedures require a healthy group environment that supports the group's benefiting and learning from a new person's perceptions. Similarly, the newcomer must use interpersonal skill in sharing her or his observations in a nonthreatening way. The ground rule is to describe observations, not make judgments. One may thus refer to tardiness by noting, "I was surprised to see that no one comes to this weekly meeting on time, and wondered when I should arrive. I've learned to come 15 minutes late like most of you, but this makes me feel uncomfortable." Contrast that statement with this one: "I was surprised to see that no one comes to this weekly meeting on time, and think this means you don't have enough respect for one another's time. I think it's a bad practice that should be stopped." A newcomer probably has not earned the right to make such strong expressions about established practices, and doing so will likely arouse defensiveness and even retaliation. At the beginning it is better for a newcomer merely to offer observations and let others decide what to do with them.

Figure 1 below shows relatively—not absolutely—how tensions rise and fall over the life of a work group.

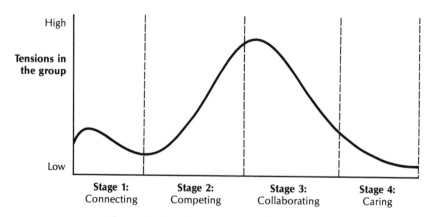

Figure 1. The stages of group development

Summary

Newcomers at work are in one of the most vulnerable phases of employment. This is a time of both substantial threat and opportunity. If the new person makes a favorable impression, he or she will form the basis for making potentially constructive contributions to the organization and increase the chances of building a successful future. With a bad start, however, all the forces that can work against the newcomer will increase the obstacles to be overcome.

Cycles of behavior seem to exist that reinforce chances of success or failure. Each favorable or unfavorable reaction tends to induce a similar response to the next behavior. The processes of entering an established, ongoing work group are among those that are less well understood. They are, however, predictable and can therefore be used to increase the chances of integrating new workers quickly and effectively. The model presented in this chapter is a framework for helping newcomers, group members, and managers increase their understanding of the issues they will face during the early, important days in which a new person enters an ongoing work group, and for helping them function more appropriately.

REFERENCE

Gussow, M. (1985, November 11). Bill Irwin: A profile. The New Yorker, pp. 51-87.

Section V.
Multiculturalism

What To Look for when Selecting a Team Building Consultant: Multicultural and Other Considerations

W. Brendan Reddy
Carol Burke

Occasionally, a personnel director, manager, or executive needs the services of an external consultant or trainer. Perhaps management has determined that team building is appropriate and desirable. Issues of productivity, climate, decision making, conflict, or human differences—such as gender and race—may have surfaced that cannot be managed and require external assistance. A secondary problem arises: "How do I know which or 'what kind' of consultant to retain?"

The consulting industry—particularly in human services, management, and interpersonal relations—is overflowing with practitioners who claim to have expertise in the area of team building. What skills does the **manager** need and what questions must the manager raise to differentiate the expert from the inexpert, the competent from the incompetent?

We have dealt with the dilemma of choosing consultants from both inside and outside organizations seeking consultants, and have generated a list of issues and questions the manager must be familiar with—and resolve—before the manager can make an informed decision about hiring an external consultant or trainer.

When the manager clearly understands the issues and problems related to selecting a team building consultant, he or she will be more likely to match the consultant's program or choice of intervention with the unique needs of the team.

This chapter highlights these issues so that readers may include them in the information gathered to use in making valid, informed

---

choices. Managing these issues is important to developing an effective team.

Two critical—and often neglected—aspects are gender and race. In building work teams, one must recognize that in both the for-profit and not-for-profit sectors, increasing numbers of women and minority group members are now employed. This chapter explores the impact of gender and race on selecting an appropriate team building consultant.

Personal background

Although one may not readily consider asking a prospective consultant about her or his personal and professional background, this is important to interactive small group work. One should explore whether the consultant has a noteworthy history in the field—and experience in industry—or whether the consultant has just recently developed a program **primarily** for entrepreneurial benefits. Although consultants' charging fees and seeking to be entrepreneurs need not necessarily be considered negative, the consultant's values should be consistent with bringing about social change. An indication of this includes the consultant's having worked through her or his own racism and sexism.

Probing these issues is quite appropriate for a client. Indeed, if the consultant treats the manager's questions as offensive, or puts up resistance, this may indicate the consultant's inexperience or failure to resolve issues.

The consulting organization

Inquiring about the consultant's organization will often produce information needing further exploration. For example, what does the consultant's advertising portray? Does it contain a philosophical statement about affirmative action or managing human differences? The more reliable organizations make their philosophical positions clear and do not hide behind public relations to attract clients.

What is the racial and gender composition of the consultant's organization? Does the consultant have access to other professionals—either within the consultant's organization or outside it—who can provide racial and gender balance to the consulting team? The client must be alert to this. Many consulting firms, agencies, and organizations have names such as "X and Associates," which often means that the consulting organization is a one- or two-person operation that **may not** have ready access to other professionals and resources. The consultant should clearly specify the operation of her or his organization and the availability of resources.

Training and experience

Closely question the prospective consultant regarding both past and current training contracts and experience. Some inexperienced or less-competent trainers and consultants readily present themselves as experts in both team building and affirmative action. The client may be particularly vulnerable to women and minority group members who claim to be experts in these areas, but base their claims only on their own race or gender. Because a manager may not have personally resolved issues concerning the dynamics of racism and/or sexism, or wants to appear "liberal," this manager may feel reluctant to ask detailed questions regarding the consultant's background and experience. One often hears the excuse "I didn't want to look sexist [or racist]."

Determine precisely what the practitioner has accomplished, where he or she has done training, and the kind of supervision provided. Merely having "experience" does not make a consultant competent. The consultant should be able to produce—upon request and within a reasonable time—letters of recommendation from current or former clients with whom the consultant has done similar work. Although confidentiality prevents you from learning details of the consulting done for other clients, you can expect a general evaluation of the consultant's work and a recommendation.

Similarly, if the consultant cannot produce consultation reports, or is vague and evasive, the manager should be suspicious and insist on documentation. Moreover, reports of the consultant's work will give the manager an idea of the consultant's thoroughness. Far too many consultants fail to deliver a final report to the client that chronicles the consultation done or provides the record and design of a training program.

Theory and concepts

Does the consultant have a theoretical framework from which he or she develops an action plan? Is the intervention design developed in a planned, rational manner and in **collaboration** with the client? Does this design rest on a solid **data base**?

The consultant who presents a team building "package" that fails to include currently gathered data; whose major contribution is a series of interventions based on "what seems to work"; who has neither a theory nor conceptual tenets, nor plans for follow-up work; and who does not understand the transfer of training simply may be an entrepreneur or someone willing to collude with the team to avoid real and substantive change.

A solid theoretical and conceptual base permits the consultant to determine when and how he or she is to intervene and at what level: organizational, group, or individual. A theoretical framework is also necessary for understanding the various "isms"—such as racism, sexism, ethnism, ageism, and the like—that seem to emerge from the interactions of work teams. One may safely assume that to have a sound conceptual base, one must read and know the literature—classic and current—and discuss the field with colleagues. The human relations field seems to have an anti-intellectual bias, and the myth persists that "doing" is all that counts; somehow, thinking and research are thought to prevent "knowing where it's at."

A theoretical and conceptual framework provides a "road map" telling the consultant where to go and when, the data needed to reach the destination, how to collect the data, what to expect along the way, when specific interventions should occur, what feedback to give to whom at what time, and how to complete an evaluation.

A framework presumes extensive knowledge of the causes, history, perpetuation, and dynamics of the "isms." Although a manager cannot readily give a written "quiz" to the prospective consultant, one should have extended discussions about the consultant's theoretical biases. Indeed, such discussions are well worth the time.

Although possessing no conceptual model from which to work is considered negative, a framework revealing biases and a philosophy the manager cannot tolerate also counts against the consultant.

Diagnosis and assessment

Expect the consultant to have a plan for gathering diagnostic data **before** he or she takes action, whether this is for training or consultation. How the consultant and her or his associates plan to conduct the diagnosis or assessment is important: Key questions must be answered **before the process begins.** Regardless of the approach, the consultant should have a "feel" for the norms and culture of the client organization and, of course, of the team. This requires a strategy for assessing and analyzing the culture of the team, if not the organization as a whole. Consequently, the consultant must be able to determine whether the team is ready— and to what degree—for **any** kind of intervention. Some consultants and trainers will intervene in any system without first determining the state of readiness. Sometimes their philosophical biases impel them to take a vociferous stand of racial and gender issues precipitously, ignorant of or insensitive to how this may leave the team in a more disrupted or agitated state than existed before the consultant entered. This is anathema to those truly seeking to promote learning or consciousness raising.

Systematic and professional assessments require a theoretical and practical knowledge of research methodology, assessment instruments, interview techniques, and observation skills. The quality of the data gathered will be commensurate with how well the assessment is planned, prepared, and executed. Raising a wide range of questions about this critical data gathering phase is quite legitimate for a manager.

Content knowledge

Although "testing" the consultant's knowledge of the field may be difficult, the manager is wise to at least "check out" the consultant's knowledge of particular content areas. Sometimes managers let themselves feel intimidated by consultants, thinking they "don't know enough" to ask intelligent questions.

Consultants who rely solely on "experience" and "gut feelings" in their consultation and workshops are typically superficial and weak in their approaches.

Orientation

Is the consultant's orientation focused on the organization, the group, or the individual? Is the change target basic policy or administrative arrangements, the attitudes and behaviors of individuals within the team, or both? The consultant who focuses on the individual may increase or heighten awareness of the issues, but if the **basic working arrangements** of the team are not changed, the effects—if any—will be short lived and will dissipate quickly. One may encounter consultants who, lacking knowledge of group structures, dynamics, and research, maintain that focusing on and working with the **individual alone** will affect the norms and operations of the team and in turn eradicate team conflicts. Little evidence supports this statement. Data, however, support the contention that changing policies, rules procedures, problem-solving techniques, administration, management, and operating mechanisms—and enforcing these changes—can lead to changed behaviors (Alvarez, Lutterman, & Associates, 1979; Livingston, 1979).

Focusing only on individuals makes success highly improbable. If the consultant is oriented toward the individual rather than toward the organization or system, the manager should view this approach as inadequate or insufficient for **long-term** organizational change.

Methods of influence

The consultant and her or his associates should be expected to have a clear idea as to how they will demonstrate to the team that it is in the members' **best interests** to change their behavior, or why changing team norms and/or processes—particularly those related to minority-group or gender issues—has a positive, useful value. Often, consultants in human resources seem stymied when asked, "Why should I change?" Anecdotal data, at least, are quite clear: If team members cannot come to see why team building is in their own best interests—not just the consultant's—they will not "buy into it."

Training

If team building is the intervention of choice, the consultant should be able to describe the design in terms of "flow"; balance of cognitive and experiential emphasis; whether simulations are packaged or "tailor made"; the use of multimedia instruction, handouts, and manuals; and, of course, a clearly defined set of objectives and how the consultant expects the participants to reach them.

Transfer of training

An issue related to the consultant's approach is how he or she proposes that the **training effects** of her or his interventions will occur. If the consultant has little or no idea, plan, or theory of how learning or change will take place and become evident in the team's daily operations, the manager would probably not want the consultant to "tinker" with the team or system. At the other extreme, if the consultant promises "magical" results with respect to what will be transferred, learned, or changed, then this consultant is not likely to be worth retaining.

Evaluation and accountability

Request from the consultant a design and a plan for **ongoing** evaluation and evaluation and feedback. This is the major way in which the consultant can demonstrate accountability. Moreover, the evaluation plan should be a priori, not post hoc. The plan for evaluation and feedback can be developed collaboratively with the team to develop ownership of, commitment to, and internal responsibility for the plan.

Expect the consultant to produce a final written report when the intervention ends. This evaluation component should be included in the original proposal and contract and negotiated as a "cost item." Item reports can also be negotiated. Agreement must be reached as to what the final report will consist of and to whom it will be sent **before** any work—including the assessment—is initiated.

Much of the above is contingent upon how the consultant and client define "success" for the team building intervention. Our experience and anecdotal evidence tell us that criteria for success are rarely articulated in any way, let alone written. Yet these criteria are obviously necessary for understanding what is to occur and the intended impact.

This discussion triggers yet another issue: Is the consultant able—and willing—to define the terms he or she may use in speaking and in written reports? For example, the terms "racism," "sexism," "institutional discrimination," "prejudice," and "bias" are frequently used synonymously by consultants, with little apparent understanding of their different meanings and implications.

Negotiating the contract

The meeting in which the contract is negotiated is important to determining if the proposed intervention will likely succeed. The contract meeting itself should provide a "model" of the consultant's work. That is, is the consultant well prepared, or lackadaisical and vague? This is when the client representative can ascertain how flexible the consultant is in matching her or his intervention or program to the unique needs of the organization. Moreover, how receptive is the consultant to the client's "input" and feedback that could change the program's design? If organizational factors require changes in the program's scope and the time required of the consultant, how will these be managed and negotiated? How does the consultant consider these factors? Flexible and collaborative consultants will be responsive without compromising their values; other consultants will balk at receiving client input, claiming it does "injustice" to their packaged programs. Although consultants surely resist clients' "taking over," typically this concern is not warranted. More frequently, the client is not permitted to give adequate input or collaborate in the design.

The system's contact person

In hiring any consultant, the client must explicitly specify **who is managing the consultant**. During contract interviews with the consultant, this client representative should test how the consultant responds to this notion. We have known consultants who, after entering an organization, answered to a senior executive instead of the team manager originally responsible for the consultant's contract. We realize that such a "switch" may occur because the consultant desires to expand her or his work in the organization. Desiring future contracts with the firm, the consultant may attempt to bypass the original contact person. This, of course, is both unprofessional and unethical. Early contract discussions, however, do help prevent this from occurring.

Summary and conclusions

We have presented conditions for selecting consultants, taking the view that the client can increase the probability of effective team building by making an informed choice. As indicated throughout this chapter, the manager and the organization will find it best to assert—and insist—that the prospective consultant(s) articulate and explicate her or his views, ideas, beliefs, values, thoughts, and feelings about her or his work. The major tool for doing this is the **intensive interview**. In addition, the manager can insist on documentation related to the consultant's other clients (recognizing that confidentiality must be maintained) and written information about the consultant's organization, orientation, and philosophy. If the client system is not satisfied, then the manager—as its representative—should not move into a contract phase; if a proposal is not sufficiently clear or detailed, it should not be signed as a contract. Once the intervention has begun, the client will find it both difficult and disruptive to stop it without having management look like "bad guys." Both the manager and client system have too much at stake in a team building program to afford anything less than an intense review of all prospective consultants.

REFERENCES

Alvarez, R., Lutterman, K.G., & Associates (1979). *Discrimination in organizations.* San Francisco: Jossey-Bass.

Livingston, J. (1979). *Fair game: Inequity and affirmative action.* San Francisco: W.H. Freeman.

E Pluribus Unum: Building Multifunctional Work Teams

Susan L. Colantuono
Ava A. Schnidman

Ours is an age of specialists. It is also a time in which the degree of collaboration among specialists often accounts for the success or failure of organizational efforts. In our work with implementing new technology, we are repeatedly involved with the start-ups of project teams comprising individuals from different functional specialties. Predictably, we have found that the issues of the multifunctional teams differ from those of intact work groups, and that the foci of team building thus must also differ.

To illustrate several of the key differences, we use the example of an implementation team whose goal was to install and test an information system. Members of this team represented five functional specialties: training, programming, systems support, users, and organization development.

Impact of functional specialties

Three issues common to multifunctional work teams are products of the diverse specialties characterizing such teams.

E pluribus unum. By bringing together many specialists to collaborate on one project, the organization acknowledges the complexity of the project. The "tunnel vision" that most specialists develop may hinder their clear understanding of what other specialists know and do. Moreover, they often do not understand fully why certain other specialists must be on the team. In our example team, the presence of users raised the eyebrows of some of the systems support specialists. After all, those from systems support knew the system and had handled implementation before. They failed to see that the users were specialists in their own organization, its politics, and its needs.

In addition to dealing with information gaps and "tunnel vision," the multifunctional work team must also meld different cognitive styles and values into an effective whole. For example, the team's programmers—who are at the top of their fields—are exceptional analytical thinkers working daily in the mode of "on/off," "black/white," "either/or." Sparks flew and confusion abounded when they met with the OD professional who dealt with the "in-process," "gray," "both/and" nuances of organizational politics, informal networks, and human motivation. These issues of creating one team from many specialties differ from those of intact work groups, whose members' skills, knowledge base, problem-solving styles, and values tend to be more homogeneous.

Who is that masked stranger? In an intact work team, members have data about their patterns of interaction. These provide grist for the team building mill. In a multifunctional work team, however, such data are usually sparse or nonexistent. Instead, stereotypes about specialists often abound. Many, for example, consider accountants to be "green-eye-shades" types, programmers to be "techies," and OD professionals to be "touchy-feely." If not addressed early, these stereotypes can prevent members from fully recognizing and using one another's strengths and abilities to contribute.

Towers of babble. Each functional specialty has its own jargon, which can lead to confusing communications among specialists. Not only are many terms unique to a given specialty (e.g., "corvus disc," "down-and-outs," "semiautonomous work groups"), but the same terms can mean different things to different specialists. In the example team, the word "systems" meant "the sum total of hardware and software" to the programmers, "existing manual paper processing" to the users, and "organizational processes" to the OD consultant. To communicate effectively in such an environment, one must literally learn new languages.

The impact of hierarchy. Another cluster of issues characterizing multifunctional work teams arises from the nature of their hierarchical structure. Unlike intact work groups, these teams comprise individuals whose reporting hierarchies are often totally unrelated. Furthermore, the members' loyalties tend to be with their management structures and only secondarily with the multifunctional work team and any designated project manager. These characteristics raise the following issues.

We cannot "kick it up the line." In most organizations, a favored strategy for resolving conflict is to "kick it up" levels of a hierarchy to the point at which reporting lines converge. With multifunctional work teams, the point of convergence is usually quite high in the organization (for the example team, this was the level of the CEO). When this is the case, team members find the kick-it-up-the-line strategy impractical. The project leader's ability to mediate conflict effectively is often hampered by the political and organizational issues that surround the work team. Therefore, the multifunctional work team is forced to find and use new strategies to resolve conflict.

Split loyalties. Members' responsibilities to a multifunctional team is only part of their jobs. Commitment to project goals may sometimes compromise the goals and integrity of a member's "home" department. This puts the member in the middle of a conflict. In the example team, the training specialists were responsible for developing and piloting a training process and related support materials for an accelerated, nationwide implementation schedule. Coming from a training department with a strong commitment to "stand-up" training, they failed to pursue other, less "people-intensive" training strategies. Because they operated in a mode consistent with their perceived responsibilities to their "home" departments, they put the ambitious implementation schedule in jeopardy. Fortunately, this problem was caught in time and remedied fairly easily. Other, more serious loyalty problems develop when a project's failure is in the vested interests of one of the departments represented on the team. This may occur, for example, when a task force explores the start-up of a new organization to replace an existing one.

Gaps and overlaps. This issue is a function of both the multiplicity of reporting relationships and the diversity of specialties. Because team members have different bases of skills and knowledge, the sum of the parts brought by members is often less than the whole required for the project. Consider the illustration in Figure 1. The circle represents the skills and responsibilities required to complete the project successfully. The team members (represented by different shapes) are inserted into the circle. Two problems are readily apparent: unfilled gaps in the project space and skill overlaps among individuals (the shaded areas). Attempts to solve the resulting conflict over who is really responsible are complicated by the cannot-kick-it-up-the-line syndrome, for there is no single manager to help clarify roles and responsibilities, as there would be in an intact work group.

These characteristics differentiating the multifunctional work team from the intact work group help determine the basic strategies of team building efforts. When we are involved in team building sessions with multifunctional teams, we focus our energy on six key goals.

Key goals of multifunctional team building

1. Clarify and reach consensus on the team's mission, goals, and roles. As must any work team, the multifunctional work group must share a common understanding of its mission, its objectives, and the roles team

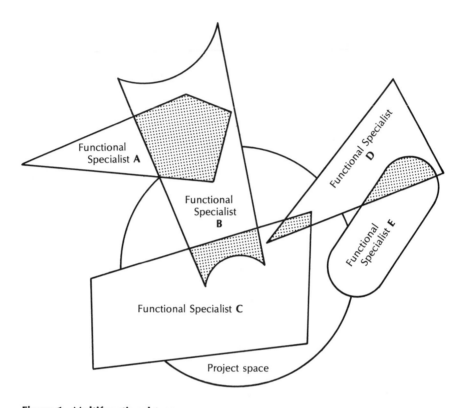

Figure 1. Multifunctional teams
(© 1984 Betty Mallott. Reprinted with permission.)

members will play in achieving this mission. Particularly important is the clarification of the leadership role (e.g., the role of the project manager). What makes the multifunctional work team different is its need for members to explore loyalty issues that might affect their performance on the team. We have found this to be most effective when team members first do this with us on a one-to-one basis to determine which issues require group discussion.

2. Analyze gaps and overlaps. A key component of clarifying roles is defining the project space and identifying any gaps or skill overlaps. Success is achieved when the team can use the process by itself whenever new gaps and/or overlaps appear. Team members find it useful to know how to differentiate between gap/overlap disputes that are structural (i.e., based on organizationally defined roles) and those that are personal (i.e., conflicts between two or more persons who want to perform the same task).

3. Unveil specialties. The process of capitalizing on team strength begins with education about bases brought to the team by other members. This also enables team members to expand their views of the project's complexity. We tend to focus on the complementary nature of the specialties represented—how they fit together—in addition to potential areas of conflict, such as different views of the world and problem-solving styles.

4. Deal with stereotypes. Team effectiveness requires team members to see the individuals behind the stereotypes. Part of this process is identifying skills and personal qualities apart from a person's technical expertise. Another part involves surfacing stereotypes, discussing their inherent facts and fallacies, and determining the ways they do or do not apply to particular members of the work team. This process helps team members establish personal contact with one another.

5. Take the babble out of the tower. Certain process interventions are intended to ease communication across specialties. These focus on encouraging members to use less jargon, developing a climate permitting members to ask for translations of terms, and educating one another in key technical terminology.

6. Empower the group. In some respects, the successful multifunctional work team operates apart from the organization. Members must rely upon themselves to resolve conflicts, marshal resources, and unblock organizational bottlenecks. Doing this requires a climate of innovation and creativity, self-sufficiency, and survival in collaboration. Members need help in finding ways to challenge the kick-it-up-the-line pattern of conflict resolution by developing alternative models, confronting the "it's-not-my-job" rigidity of formal organization structures by supporting risk taking, and rejecting the "we-don't-have-the-resources" argument by teaching creative problem solving.

Conclusions

Achieving these six goals is an ideal worth striving toward. Pressures of time, management expectations, and project demands often conspire against fully realizing all six goals. What **is** important is recognizing the unique characteristics of the multifunctional work team and tailoring the team building efforts to meet the team's most pressing needs.

Whenever organizational goals rely on collaboration across specialties, multifunctional teams will abound. Whenever consultants and managers recognize the difference between these teams and intact work teams, they will contribute to the success of the multifunctional team and the organization.

Moving a Team to Multiculturalism

Frederick A. Miller

Team building in America is essentially a white man's invention, because most organizations—particularly at their middle and upper levels—have historically been composed almost entirely of white men.

Times are changing, and so is the appearance of organizations. White women and men and women of color are finally achieving positions of influence within corporate America. They have integrated the ranks of the decision makers.

Suddenly, team building is no longer a process **of** white men **for** white men. Organization staffs are being called upon to find ways of working effectively with the "new person." We consultants are the "experts" charged with helping staffs adjust to these changes. Too often, however, we fail to recognize all but the most blatant examples of racism and sexism among those we seek to help. We thus inadvertently support monocultural norms and behaviors instead of helping staffs develop new ways of team building. This chapter examines some of the issues related to these changes.

Team norms

Every team develops and operates according to its own set of norms, or acceptable patterns of behavior, such as "Don't make waves," "Speak only in a calm voice," "Avoid revealing personal feelings," "Sexist and ethnic jokes are okay," "Sports and military analogies are the right ways to communicate." These norms have been adopted by many teams of white men.

Adding a new person, however, brings to the team cultural values and behaviors different from those of the white men already on staff. In the early 1960s when corporations first began allowing blacks to assume

---

lower-level management positions—without decision-making authority—and in the 1970s when white women started moving up the corporate ladder, many thought that despite the new faces business could continue as usual. The theory behind this assumption was that one could treat everyone entering the corporation the way one treats white men. People pretended that nothing had changed. But things had changed. The appearance of the new person created strong pressures: pressures on the new person to change, on the team to change its norms.

When persons come together to form a team, they develop patterns of communication. Long-established norms of the all-white, male team must be modified to allow for differences associated with color or gender. For example, when a white person disagrees with someone, he or she is less likely to be confrontational than would a black person in similar circumstances. Similarly, men tend to regard crying as a signal that someone is out of control, whereas women often cry as a natural expression of anger or frustration. Whether the new person is a person of color or a white woman, to succeed in the job this person must be accepted and appreciated for her or his own unique qualities.

Teams often operate using majority rule, which can prove effective when the majority understands and acts in the best interests of **all** of its members. When a new person joins the team, however, the dynamics of team building change significantly. Members may not **know** which actions, behaviors, and attitudes are in the new person's best interests. Bringing to the team their own biases, members may simply not recognize racism or sexism operating within the team, or their own collusion regarding these issues. They may not notice, for example, that all the blacks in their organization hold only low-level positions, that women are ignored or interrupted during meetings, that blacks get left out of the communications loop, and that secretaries are expected to serve coffee and wait on their managers.

New persons face a "lose/lose" situation. They can either support the decisions of the majority that they recognize as racist or sexist, or they can dispute them. Doing either sets new persons apart from the team, focusing attention on their color and/or gender and how it differs from that of the majority.

It is time to redefine team play

"Team play" has often meant going along with the majority, even when you disagree with what this is. We must recognize, however, that someone can still be a team member while opposing the team on certain issues. Commitment to cultural values not shared by white men should not stigmatize a new person as a defector from the team. Being critical is not necessarily the same as being disloyal.

Team play is better defined more broadly as trying to do what is right to accomplish business, whether this is in support of or **in spite of** the majority.

Addressing racism and sexism

Teams comprising only white mean often feel they have addressed racism and/or sexism merely by hiring the new person. They often think this indicates they are not prejudiced, and that the team may now continue with business as usual.

This is not so, for the need for team members to address their own racism and sexism has just begun. During the hiring process, the team may have been forced to recognize for the first time its feelings of racism or sexism. Now, by including the new person on the team, team members must confront their own and others' racism and sexism.

The issues change from asking "Do we want this person who is so obviously different from us to be on our team?" to asking "Am I willing to share power with the new person? How much of my white male cultural norms am I willing to modify to work with the new person?"

In both the work place and at home, team members will be drawn into discussions about the new person. They will interact with the new person in various work situations, both one on one and in the company of other organization members. Racist or sexist remarks and jokes, which may have become an accepted part of the work environment, now take on a new meaning and team members must decide whether to confront those who repeat such remarks or allow them to be made.

While the white male team wrestles with these issues, the new persons are not immune to racism and sexism. Often they wonder, "Is it them or me?" When new persons feel victimized by the attitudes of other team members, they often ask, "Am I being oversensitive? Is it my imagination that I'm being mistreated, or is it really someone else's racism [and/or sexism]? Or is it my **own** racism [and or sexism] causing me to feel this way?" Men of color tend to assume the other person(s) is at fault; women tend to blame themselves. No matter who the new person is, however, to become an effective member that person must acknowledge her or his own prejudices, especially those relating to white men.

How costly is the price of admission?

Team membership always bears a price tag, but for white women and persons of color, joining an all-white-male team can be expensive indeed.

Frequently the price is to become, as much as possible, a white man. The more the new person's dress, hair style, speech patterns, work attitudes, family values, political beliefs, and attitudes toward the team imitate those of white men, the better the new person will fit in. For women, this may mean wearing tailored suits rather than "feminine" dresses. For persons of color, this may mean no "Afro" hair styles or black slang.

This forces new persons to make tough decisions. How much of one's own identity is one willing to surrender to join the team? Are color and gender differences really important, or are they merely incidental and therefore not worth trying to maintain?

Most teams are not aware that they demand such a high price for membership. The new person may not recognize this, either—at least not at first. But new persons begin to sense this as they experience the inner conflict accompanying the attempt to deny a part of oneself.

Reordering the pecking order

The pecking order changes, however imperceptibly, each time someone joins the team. This change is always more visible when the new member is a white woman or person of color.

New issues—such as favoritism—will arise that would not come up were the new member a white man. Is the new person getting special consideration merely because of being different? Sexism can take the form of the manager's giving "different" attention to the newcomer. Sometimes attention given to a woman may stem from physical attraction or prejudices about the "weaker sex." Racism can prompt a manager to fear a lawsuit should a person of color fail or to wonder if such persons need more training or direct supervision than white persons.

Even if a manager spends the same amounts of time interacting with the new person as with other team members, the team may assume the new person is getting more attention because this person is so visible. If the manager pays less attention to the new person, the new person may assume he or she is disliked simply for being different.

Confused messages about a manager's attitude toward the new person scramble everyone's sense of that person's—and one's own—place in the pecking order. The manager is primarily responsible for dealing with racism or sexism associated with the new person's addition to the team, a difficult task best accomplished by encouraging open discussion among all team members. A manager's efforts to manage racism and sexism will have their own influence on the pecking order. The time spent dealing with these issues will be viewed as a measure of the new person's importance.

In search of a superstar

No manager wants to hire new persons doomed to fail because they are ill equipped to deal with the extra pressures of racism and sexism.

Therefore, a manager may hire someone who is overqualified, a "superstar" clearly superior in skills, knowledge, or education to white men being hired for comparable positions. After all, superstars have a better chance of succeeding at the three jobs asked of them: satisfying the requirements of the announced job, establishing new norms allowing someone other than a white man to succeed, and educating other team members about the problems faced by white women and/or persons of color in the work place. Struggling to do these three jobs results in stress, anger, and burnout.

This desire to ensure a new person a "good" opportunity for success creates several problems. Because the manager has hired a new person overqualified for the position, this person soon begins to look for additional responsibilities or a more challenging position. Because the new person "knows" he or she is qualified for a higher position, this person can easily imagine that all barriers to promotion are racist and/or sexist.

Bringing in a superstar upsets the status quo and may result in other team members' charging reverse discrimination and racism and/or sexism. When one hires a new person, one must seriously examine the problems of racism and/or sexism existing within the team and the organization. If these discomforting issues are tackled before the new person arrives, that person may be able to avoid being the focus of the issues and the object of strong negative feelings. The new person thus may not have to work three jobs instead of just one. The team's norms may have already been altered enough to allow someone other than a white man to succeed. Unfortunately, it is often the job of changing the white man's norms that burns out the new person.

So who asked to be a pioneer?[1]

Many persons of color and white women entering management during the mid-1960s knew they were going to be the first such persons to hold those positions in their organizations. They knew the road was uncharted and expected to encounter racism or sexism, perhaps even more than what their parents encountered. Few were disappointed.

Many discovered that racism and sexism posed insurmountable barriers to their success. Some turned to other endeavors. Some struggled endlessly with no success. Some celebrated small achievements and remained to continue struggling, but with lowered expectations. A few achieved grand things. All knew they were pioneers and accepted that being a forerunner meant paying a high price.

Times have changed. Some persons have declared the struggle over racism and sexism a dead issue. They feel that the success a white woman or person of color can achieve is limited only by that person's talent and efforts.

Many white women and persons of color have seen themselves achieve heights that people in the 1960s considered impossible. A few have parents who have attained high social stature and economic success. They have heard of "sit-ins," Jim Crow, grandfather clauses, riots, and famous black persons' winning Nobel Prizes, but they did not belong to the "movement." That was before their time.

Many of these persons are now becoming the first of their gender or color to assume positions of authority on previously all-white-male staffs. They merely want to do their jobs and to succeed or fail on their own talents. No one told them about the frontiers of racism and sexism still waiting to be conquered. No one told them they would be the new pioneers.

Part of these new persons' struggle, therefore, is to recognize they may pay a price for being pioneers. Their work could include supporting their managers in addressing issues of racism and/or sexism, or even taking the lead in this should their managers be inadequate at this task. Being unprepared for these realities will make the new person's entry onto the team that much harder. And if, after joining the team, this person fails to point out instances of sexism and racism, the team will have a false feeling of comfort regarding these issues.

Organizations continue to change dramatically. Teams are becoming more culturally diverse. Increasingly, color and gender are being recognized as work-related issues that must be discussed and resolved by the work unit. In some organizations, the white woman or person of color is no longer forced to imitate white men; the cultural norms and behaviors of women, blacks, Hispanics, Asians, Native Americans, and East Indians are recognized and accepted as different from one another and from those of white men. Unfortunately, such organizations remain the exception, not the rule.

America is a "stew" of cultures. To maximize the competitive edge this can provide, we must value and use our differences and what we have in common.

In view of all these changes, team building has become a vital art. It is the human vehicle by which organizations can achieve multiculturalism. Consultants seeking to facilitate these changes must always be vigilant in addressing the presence of racism and sexism—in team members, the new person, and themselves.

NOTE

1. I first heard this concept discussed in a conversation with Daryl Funches, Charles Coverdale, and David Thomas at NTL Institute's setting in Bethel, Maine.

Biographical Sketches of the Contributors

John D. Adams, Ph.D. is director of Eartheart Enterprises, Inc., an international consulting and training firm. He is a member of the American Psychological Association and of NTL Institute. Dr. Adams's primary interests are stress management, health promotion, leadership development, and performance enhancement. He lectures and consults widely in these areas and has written an extensive list of related books and articles.

Gene Bocialetti, Ph.D. is an assistant professor of organizational behavior at the Whittemore School of Business and Economics at the University of New Hampshire. He has done consulting work in such areas as authority relations in organizations, adult career development, small group process, and organizational diagnosis and change, and was heavily involved in Ford Motor Company's implementation of its quality of work life program. Dr. Bocialetti is a member of the Academy of Management, the Organizational Behavior Teaching Society, and NTL Institute.

Nancy L. Brown is an independent consultant based in Cincinnati who works in organization design and redesign, "just-in-time" manufacturing, total quality systems, management development, and multicultural work place development. Prior to establishing her practice, she was marketing manager and then consultant for Procter & Gamble. She is a member of NTL Institute.

Carol Burke is corporate personnel manager for Digital Equipment Corporation and a member of NTL Institute.

W. Warner Burke, Ph.D. is professor of psychology and education and coordinator of the Graduate Program in Organizational Psychology at Teachers College, Columbia University. He is also president of W. Warner Burke Associates, Inc. Dr. Burke is editor of *Academy of Management Executive*, a member of the American Psychological Association, and of the board of governors of both the Academy of Management and the American Society for Training and Development. He has written 10 books and more than 50 articles on organization development, training, social and organizational psychology, and conference planning, and is a diplomate in industrial/organization psychology, American Board of Professional Psychology.

Richard E. Byrd, Ph.D. is known for his pioneering work in the human factors of risk taking and applications of management research and theory to organizational effectiveness. He has directed his own consulting firm since 1966, and has authored more than 50 books, articles, and audiotapes. Dr. Byrd is a member of the American Psychological Association, the Psychological Association of Minnesota and of the District of Columbia, and of NTL Institute. He is a founding member and former president of the Association for Creative Change, and is a licensed clergyman in the Episcopal Diocese of Minnesota.

Susan L. Colantuono is a partner in the DELTECH Consulting Group, specializing in the role of human factors in the design and implementation of automated systems. She works with information systems departments in modifying both their strategies and processes for designing systems that will be successful for their users. In addition, she works with organizations on issues of management development, team building, and career development, and has written several articles and *Build Your Career*, a career management workbook. She is a member of NTL Institute.

Kathleen D. Dannemiller has been involved in training and development for more than 25 years and is a member of NTL Institute. For 12 years she worked as an internal consultant and teacher at the University of Michigan, then started her own company with Charles Tyson, operating out of Ann Arbor, Michigan. Her current primary clients include Ford Motor Company, Pillsbury, and Michigan Bell Telephone.

Allan B. Drexler, Ph.D. is president of Drexler & Associates, Inc. of Annapolis, Maryland, and since 1971 has consulted to businesses seeking organizational and strategic change. He has developed organization-wide OD programs for General Mills, ARA Food Services, the U.S. Naval Academy, and the International Monetary Fund, among others. His current work has been on team performance and effectiveness at all levels in the organization. Dr. Drexler is a member of NTL Institute and a lecturer in the NTL/American University master's degree program in human resources development.

Russell H. Forrester, Ph.D. is a psychologist who directs selection and performance management programs for a major agency of the federal government. His 16 years of experience in human resource management as a manager and consultant has centered on developing organizational systems that tap employee potential, increase job satisfaction, resolve conflicts, and enhance productivity. Dr. Forrester has designed and staffed numerous workshops for senior managers—including those presented by NTL Institute—and has lectured at various universities and professional associations.

Herman Gadon, Ph.D. is director of Executive Programs for Scientists and Engineers at the University of California, San Diego. He has been a faculty member or lecturer at universities around the world. Dr. Gadon is the coauthor of *Effective Behavior in Organizations* and *Alternative Work Schedules*, which in 1979 received the Annual Best Book Award of the American Society of Personnel, and his pioneering articles on flexible working hours helped introduce the concept to the United States. He is a member of NTL Institute, the National Labor Panel, and the National Public Disputes Panel of the American Arbitration Association, and is a charter member of the Society of Professionals in Dispute Resolution.

Robert T. Golembiewski, Ph.D. fills two professional roles: research professor at the University of Georgia in Athens, Georgia, and distinguished visiting professor at the University of Calgary in Alberta, Canada. He has published across the behavioral and management sciences, and his 47th book is *Stress in Organizations*. Dr. Golembiewski has also authored more than 250 articles and case studies. He is a member of NTL Institute.

Philip G. Hanson, Ph.D. is currently chief of Psychology Service at the Medical Center of Houston, Texas, and associate professor of psychology at the Baylor College of Medicine and the University of Houston. A member of NTL Institute, he has been associated with that organization since 1964.

Kaleel Jamison was president of Kaleel Jamison Associates and the Living School. A consultant to business organizations and a human relations trainer for more than 18 years, she developed a methodology addressing human development concerns on a system-wide basis. She specialized in competition, communication, conflict management, career planning, personal growth, management development, and improving work relationships among people of different colors, genders, and cultures. Ms. Jamison was accredited by Certified Consultants International and a member of NTL Institute, for whom she staffed professional and managerial development seminars. Her articles appeared in numerous professional journals, and her book on leadership, self-empowerment, and personal growth, *The Nibble Theory and the Kernel of Power*, was published in 1984 by Paulist Press. She died August 30, 1985.

Bernard Lubin, Ph.D. is a professor of psychology, medicine, and administration and director of the Doctoral Program in Community Psychology at the University of Missouri at Kansas City. He is a member of NTL Institute, a diplomate in clinical psychology (American Board of

Professional Psychology), and a fellow of the American Psychological Association and the Association for the Advancement of Science. Dr. Lubin is the author of more than 180 published works, including six books.

Frederick A. Miller is president of Kaleel Jamison Associates, and has worked as an organization development consultant and human relations trainer for 14 years. His special interests include designing and implementing innovative approaches for developing people at all levels of an organization and improving work relationships among people of color and whites, and between men and women. A member of NTL Institute, he recently served on that organization's board of directors and is on the board of the Organization Development Network.

Jane Moosbruker, Ph.D. is an organization development consultant from Bolton, Massachusetts. In private practice for more than 15 years, she consults primarily to "high-tech" and medical systems, focusing on the management of change, organizational structure, open systems planning, team building, and conflict. Dr. Moosbruker has taught psychology at Boston College and in the School of Dental Medicine at Harvard University. She is a member of NTL Institute, the Academy of Management, the Massachusetts Public Health Association, the Society for the Psychological Study of Social Issues, and the Organization Development Network.

Judith Palmer, Ph.D. has worked since 1978 as a human resources development consultant in a Fortune 500 Corporation, and previously as an independent consultant in the Greater Boston area. She was cofounder and partner of a consulting firm that continues to specialize in organizational and multicultural effectiveness, and has been on the staff of a university counseling center. Dr. Palmer is a member of NTL Institute.

Thomas H. Patten, Jr., Ph.D. has written more than 80 articles and authored or edited eight major books. His work covers most aspects of human resources management. Dr. Patten has consulted in personnel, compensation, organization development, training, human resource planning, and equal opportunity to clients in industry and government in the U.S. and Europe. He has also been a court-appointed master in chancery and expert witness and consultant in some of the leading cases in the U.S. involving alleged sex discrimination, improper conducting of wage and salary surveys, and unjust dismissals stemming from improper performance appraisals. He is a member of NTL Institute.

W. Brendan Reddy, Ph.D. is director of the Institute for Consultation and Training at the University of Cincinnati, where he is a professor of psychology. He is a member of the American Psychological Association and NTL Institute. Dr. Reddy's primary interests are organization development, process consultation, team building, training, and third-party intervention. He has consulted, taught, researched, and written in these areas, and co-edited the recent book *Training Theory and Practice*.

Eva Schindler-Rainman, DSW, is an internationally known consultant based in Los Angeles, California. She is a member of NTL Institute.

Ava A. Schnidman is a partner in the DELTECH Consulting Group, through which she focuses on helping organizations maximize productivity by working on both their social and technical systems. She has been an organization development consultant and line manager for more than 13 years, and her clients have included manufacturing, financial services, and hospitality industry organizations and government agencies. In addition to sociotechnical work, she also specializes in managing complex organizational change, team development, and management education. A member of NTL Institute, she has published articles in several journals.

David Sibbet is an organization consultant, facilitator, and conceptual designer. His company, Sibbet & Associates, is pioneering the use of interactive media for team building, strategic communications, and organization development. He produces graphic guides on group process, formal models, and planning instruments that help companies integrate their core planning, management, and development processes. Companies that have used these processes include Apple Computer, Lukas Films, and Procter and Gamble. He has also designed experiential educational programs focusing on leadership development.

Marvin R. Weisbord, an organization development consultant since 1969, is senior vice president of Block, Petrella, Weisbord, a consulting firm specializing in participative reorganization, work redesign, and starting new facilities. He has consulted with many corporations in business, industry, banking, and health care in many countries. A member of NTL Institute, Certified Consultants International, and the European Institute for Transnational Studies, he has written widely on the theory and practice of organizational change and for six years was an associate editor of *The Journal of Applied Behavioral Science*. His latest book is entitled *Productive Workplaces: Organizing and Managing for Dignity, Meaning, and Community*.